1

Trailblazing Women

Their Trek to the California Gold Rush

Alton Pryor

Trailblazing Women

Their Trek to the California Gold Rush

Copyright © Alton Pryor 2016
ISBN: 978-0-692-55427-2
Library of Congress Control No.: 2015916871

Stagecoach Publishing
5360 Campcreek Loop
Roseville, CA. 95747
916-771-8166
stagecoach@surewest.net
www.stagecoachpublishing.com

Forward

The California Gold Rush was the largest mass migration in American history since it brought some 300,000 people to California.

It all started on January 24, 1848, when James W. Marshall found gold on his piece of land at Sutter's Mill in Coloma. The news of gold quickly spread.

People from Oregon, Sandwich Islands (now Hawaii) and Latin America were the first to hear the breaking news, so they were the first to arrive in order to test their luck in California.

Soon, others from the rest of the United States, Europe, Australia and China followed. Since they arrived during 1849 they were called the "forty-niners".

Table of Contents

1

The Early Arrivals

The arrival of women in California during the Gold Rush was indeed a strange occurrence. Sierra Foothills Magazines said one young man wrote:

> *"Got nearer to a woman this evening than I have been in six months. Came near fainting."*

In 1850, the number of females in California was placed at about eight percent of the population. Widows or single women didn't remain that way very long.

Some women trekked to the Gold Fields alone.

A Sonora storekeeper said that one widow buried her husband one day and married the chief mourner the next.

Women in the California Gold Rush were scarce but played an important role. Some of the first people in the mining fields were wives and families that were already in California. These women and their children worked right alongside the men.

Men in the gold fields coming from other states generally left their wives and families at home. As travel arrangements improved and made it easier for women to travel, the California female population increased steadily.

Most women coming to California came aboard paddle wheel steamers by way of Panama. While this trip took 40 to 90 days, it was one of the fastest ways to travel to the California gold fields.

It was expensive, costing $400 to $600 per person for a one-way ticket.

The Great Potato Famine in Ireland (1845-1852) caused mass starvation, disease and emigration. It drove many desperate women to the United States and to California.

Women were in great demand in those days. Steamboat agents were known to cry out, "Ladies on board" when a boat arrived at its California destination.

In a gold camp in Coloma, one man owned a woman's fashionable boot. He was so proud of his treasure that he would sometimes exhibit it, charging $1 per person to look upon the object. He had plenty of takers. "The chunk ain't found that can buy this boot! 'Taint for sale, no-how."

Word of the shortage of women made its way to France, and several companies of girls of good character landed in San Francisco. They were hired by gamblers and saloon-keepers at the outrageous sum of $250 a month to sit beside the croupier and rake in the winnings.

Some were sent to the bar to dispense drinks. While their employers guarded them with vigilance, as their presence did indeed increase business, within a week or so most of them had husbands. When news of their success sped back to France, women of a less savory sort set sail for the gold fields.

The San Francisco newspaper, *The Pacific News*, announced in the October 1850 issue that nine hundred of the French women were expected. That announced shipment dwindled to only 50 such arrivals.

It didn't take long for the bordello girls to set up for business in the Gold Camps.

Women then started arriving from other parts of the world, the Marquesas, Peru and Australia among many. These women hurried to the gold camps and prospered wherever they settled.

One prostitute claimed to have made $50,000 in just a few months. A sad report is that some Native American women were victimized and passed around freely in the gold camps.

Enos Christman was an early-day newspaperman. On August 9, 1851, he wrote:

"I feel that I am a rover, a wanderer
on the face of the earth. In a land

flowing, not with milk and honey, but with flapjacks and gold dust, far from home and kindred, and surrounded by the offscourings and scum of society, from all parts of the habitable globe. All selfish, each for himself, and his Satanic Majesty for all, I have scarcely met with a half a dozen respectable women, or men with their families since I left the Atlantic States.

"The women of other nations, what few there are, are nearly all lewd harlots, who are drunk half of the time, or sitting behind a gambling table dealing monte. To see a woman who can read and write is a curiosity. Indeed, the majority of our females are a disgrace to woman. All are ruined."

Still some communities celebrated the members of the world's oldest profession. On Valentine's Day, the city of Jackson gathered to honor the bawdy house girls and their profession, which was legalized in 1854.

Town leaders set a heart-shaped plaque in a cement slab near several deteriorating buildings that had once housed prostitutes.

Not all townspeople enjoyed the merits of the plaque. One was heard to say, "Next, we need a plaque to commemorate bootlegging in the city."

Even women of good reputation made money in the gold rush camps. Sarah Royce was one of the first women in the gold field. She was surprised when a boarding house owner offered her one hundred dollars a month to cook three meals a day for his boarders.

The job came without any dishwashing duties and had help to assist her with the cooking.

There is the story of the inveterate bachelor who married a spinster because she refused to wash his clothes for him. He was determined that she should do it at any price.

Dame Shirley, whose real name was Louise Amelia Knapp Smith Clapp, wrote in one of her letters, "Everybody ought to go to the mines just to see how little it takes to make people comfortable in the world."

Dame Shirley wrote 23 letters from September 13, 1851 to November 21, 1852, which were published in a short-lived literary journal, *The Pioneer: a California Monthly Magazine.*

Her letters described life at Rich Bar and nearby Indian Bar on the east branch of the North Fork of the Feather River. Among those who read the series of letters was Brett Harte, who wrote *The Luck of Roaring Camp.*

Women in the gold camps were determined to be either "good" or "bad". The arrival of the first good woman in the mining town of Columbia, according to Sierra Foothills Magazine.com, was marked by a parade and brass band.

Women didn't hesitate to denote which class of femininity they belonged. Big Annie, a well-known prostitute in Columbia pushed the town's school marm into the street.

The town's firemen decided this wasn't right. They dragged their water cart to Big Annie's place and washed her out of the building.

In woman-starved California, it wasn't unusual for a man to pay up to $16 to $20 a night for the privilege of having a woman sit at the same gaming table with them.

In San Francisco initially, women and men both were housed in wooden houses. These included ships hauled up on the shore to serve as homes or businesses, canvas wood framed tents, and other highly flammable structures.

These structures, combined with a lot of drunken gamblers and miners led to many fires. Most of San Francisco burned down six times in great fires between 1849 and 1852.

Young Chinese girls were bought in China and sold as Chinese prostitutes for Chinese men. They were considered the bottom of the prostitute's hierarchy. Hispanic women were considered one rung above the Chinese women.

California prostitutes suffered from a litany of problems common to the trade. Unwanted pregnancy was a real possibility since there were no contraceptive drugs or apparatus available.

The alternative to such unwanted abortions was a backroom abortion or giving birth and raising an illegitimate child of often uncertain parentage.

Disease was a constant problem. Syphilis was common among both men and women. Treatment was costly and painful. Other communicable diseases were cholera, measles, tuberculosis and diphtheria.

Professional medical training and certification was just starting to be developed. Medical knowledge was so poor that training did little or no good. If you survived, you got a doctor bill. If you died, you got buried.

2

Luzena Wilson

Luzena Wilson

Her husband, Mason Wilson, wanted to head for the gold fields immediately. But Luzena Stanley Wilson would not be left behind, even with two small children in tow.

"I thought, where he could go so could I, and where I went I could take my two little toddling babies."

Luzena soon realized the task she had undertaken. "If I had, I think I should still be in my log cabin in Missouri. When we talked it over, it seemed like such a small task to go out to California and once we were there, fortune would come to us."

The Wilsons gave no thought to selling their section of land in Missouri. They simply left their two years of labor behind for the next newcomer. "Monday, we would be off."

As they looked over their belongings, they decided to throw aside anything not absolutely necessary. Beds they would need along with food to eat.

"It was a strange but comprehensive load we stowed away in our prairie schooner. Some things which we thought were necessities when we started became burdensome luxuries. Many were dropped along the roadside."

Included in the things Luzena decided she could live without on the trail were a number of pots and kettles. "For bacon and flour it requires but few vessels to cook them."

One luxury the Wilson's did have was a "muley" cow. Luzena refused to give up this animal. "She followed our train across the desert, shared our food and water, and our fortunes, good or ill, and lived in California to a serene old age."

The Wilsons found their first day was slow getting them to the Missouri River. At the river, they were ferried across and made their first camp site.

Luzena refused to leave her muley cow behind. The cow crossed the desert in good shape and provided fresh milk for her babies.

The wagon train was now in Indian Territory and commenced Luzena's first terrors. "Around us in every direction were groups of Indians sitting, standing and on horseback. There were as many as 200 in the camp.

The Indians were friendly and swapped ponies for whiskey and tobacco. When the wagon train departed the following day, Luzena said she sheltered her babies with her own body, waiting for imaginary arrows to pierce her body.

The next night's campsite was again surrounded by Indians. Luzena asked her husband, Mason, to ask the neighboring camp, which was the Independence Company., if they could join them for protection. Their neighbors sent word back that they didn't want to be bothered with women and children because they were on their way to California.

"My anger at their insulting answer roused my courage, and my last fear of Indians died a sudden death. I am only a woman," I said, "but I am going to California, too, and without the help of the Independence Company."

Luzena described the trip. "Day after day, week after week, we went through the same weary routine of breaking camp at daybreak, yoking the oxen and cooking our meagre rations over a fire of sagebrush and scrub oak. We packed up again, washed our coffeepot and camp-kettle and scanty wardrobe in the little streams we crossed, and struck camp again at sunset."

While the Wilson's safely forged the Platte River in Nebraska, a wagon behind them was not so lucky. The Platte River is known for its quicksand.

We turned to watch the frantic driver in the wagon behind us shout and whip his beleaguered animals in vain. The treacherous sand gave way under the animals' feet. They sank slowly, gradually but surely. They went out of sight inch by inch and the water rose over the moaning beasts.

The road was lined with skeletons of the poor beasts who died in the struggle to get to California. "Sometimes we found bones of men bleaching beside their broken-down and abandoned wagons."

Once the Wilsons arrived in Sacramento, Luzena learned the value of being a female minority in a male-dominated group.

A hungry miner approached her while she was cooking dinner for her family. He offered her five dollars for her biscuits. When Luzena hesitated to respond, the miner upped the offer to ten dollars. She gladly accepted.

The Wilsons sold their oxen to purchase a stake in a hotel. The hotel consisted of two rooms, the kitchen and a living room. During her six month stay in Sacramento, Luzena saw only two other women.

Around Christmas time in 1850, the levies around Sacramento broke and the floodwaters damaged the Wilson's property and their small fortune of barley. Terrified of the long duration of winter, the Wilson's learned of gold strikes in Nevada City.

Luzena found a man with a wagon and team who said he would take her and her children to Nevada City for $700. She agreed to pay it if she survived the journey and made any money.

On arrival in Nevada City, Luzena saw a sign for the Wamac Hotel. She decided she would open a rival hotel and take in boarders as a source of income. She chopped wood and drove stakes into the ground.

By the time her husband returned in the evening, she had 20 men eating at her table in the El Dorado Hotel. In six weeks, she had enough money to pay off the teamster that had brought her and her family to Nevada City.

After eighteen weeks in Nevada City, the Wilsons suffered another setback. Fire swept through Nevada City, burning the El Dorado Hotel to the ground.

They journeyed back to Sacramento, but decided it wasn't what they wanted. They traveled further up the valley to the foothills of what is now Vacaville.

While Mason set off to find a job cutting hay, the industrious Luzena created a sign from scrap lumber, saying: Wilson's Hotel. Luzena remained in Vacaville for 27 years.

Luzena died at age 83 of thyroid cancer on July 11, 1902, at the Hotel Pleasanton in San Francisco.

3

Dame Shirley's Letters

Louise Amelia Knapp Smith Clapp may have impacted Gold Rush history more than any other woman. During her time in the California Gold Rush, she wrote a series of letters to her sister Molly in New England.

Twenty three of her letters, under the nom de plume "Dame Shirley" were published in the short-lived literary journal, *The Pioneer: A California Monthly Magazine.*

She was born in New Jersey in 1819. Her father, Moses Smith, died when she was 13 years old, and her mother, Lois, died five years later. Louise was entrusted to a family friend, an attorney named Osmyn Baker.

He sent Louise to school at the Female Seminary in Charlestown, Massachusetts and to Amherst Academy. Her closest sibling was Mary Jane, or "Molly" to whom she later wrote her famous Gold Rush letters.

She was impressed with meeting Alexander Hill Everett, a widely traveled diplomat while traveling by stagecoach in southern Vermont. Louise was a 20-year-old student.

She became fascinated by Everett in an academic way and exchanged letters with him even though he was 30 years her elder. He once advised her, "If you were to add to the love of reading the habit of writing you would find a new and inexhaustible source of comfort and satisfaction opening upon you."

She accepted his advice but rejected his love. She married Fayette Clapp, a medical student and doctor's apprentice who was five years her junior.

Both longed to go west. When it was announced that gold was discovered in California, they packed their trunks and boarded the schooner *Manilla*.

When they arrived in San Francisco five months later, the foggy and damp weather did not agree with Fayette. He suffered from bilious attacks, fever, ague and jaundice.

Louise on the other hand, liked the city. She wrote: "What with its many-costumed, many-tongued, many-visaged population, its flashy looking squares, built one day and burned the next; its wickedly beautiful gambling houses; its gay stores where the richest productions of every nation can be found; and its wild, free unconventional style of living, it possesses, for the young adventurer especially, a strange charm."

For health reasons, the couple moved inland, settling in Plumas City. Louise described this town as a "was to have been city of vanishing splendors." Plumas City, which was erected near the Feather

River between Sacramento and Marysville, no longer exists.

Fayette next set out with a friend for Rich Bar, hoping the pure air would improve his health. He also hoped there was a shortage of doctors there.

Luckily, he found there was indeed a shortage of doctors. Once he established himself, he returned to Plumas City for his wife.

Louise found there were few women, only four besides herself, at Rich Bar. The town had no brothel, although the Empire, a combination inn, restaurant and general store had originally been constructed with a brothel in mind.

The venture failed and was sold out to Curtis and Louise Bancroft for a few hundred dollars. Louise Bancroft was referred to in the Dame Shirley letters as Mrs. B.

Mrs. B was the first woman Louise Clapp met at Rich Bar. When Louise Clapp entered the Empire, Mrs. Bancroft was cooking supper for a half-dozen people while her two week old son lay screaming in his "champagne basket".

In her second Dame Shirley letter, Louise wrote about the first woman to arrive in Rich Bar. She was called "The Indiana Girl."

"The sweet name of *girl* seems sadly incongruous when applied to such a gigantic piece of humanity...The far-off roll of her mighty voice, booming through two closed doors and a long entry, added greatly to the severe attack of nervous headache under which I was suffering when she called. This gentle creature wears the thickest kind of miner's boots, and has the dainty habit of wiping her dishes on her apron! Last spring she walked to this place and packed fifty pounds of flour on her back down that awful hill—the snow being five feet deep at the time.

"All the same, several men, including Yank, keeper of a log cabin store further up the bar, were smitten with the charms of the Indiana Girl. He takes me largely into his confidence, as to the various ways he has of doing green miners.

"As for his log cabin store, it is the most comical olla podrida (potpourri) of heterogeneous merchandise that I ever saw. There is nothing you can ask for but what he has—from crowbars down to cambric needles; from velveteen trowsers up to broadcloth coats of the jauntiest description...His collection of novels is by far the largest, the greasiest and the yellowest kivered (covered) of any to be found on the river."

In a later letter, Louise describes the log cabin that her husband Fayette acquired on the sparsely populated Indian Bar, upriver from Rich Bar but within walking distance.

"Enter my dear; you are perfectly welcome; besides, we could not keep you out if we would, as there is not even a latch on the canvas door...The room into which we have now entered is about twenty feet square.

"It is lined over the top with white cotton cloth...the sides are hung with a gaudy chintz, which I consider a perfect marvel of calico printing. The artist seems to have exhausted himself on roses...from earliest budhood up to the ravishing beauty of the 'last rose of summer'.

"A curtain of the above described chintz divides off a portion of the room, behind which stands a bedstead. The fireplace is built of stones and mud, the chimney finished off with alternate layers of rough sticks. The mantlepiece is formed of a beam of wood, covered with strips of tin procured from cans, upon which still remain in black hieroglyphics, the names of the different eatables which they formerly contained.

"I suppose that it would be no more than civil to call a hole two feet square in one side of the room, a window, although it is as yet guiltless of glass."

The path from Indian Bar to Rich Bar, where Fayette Clapp had his office was precarious. Footbridges across the river were felled logs still wrapped in bark and moss. Large rocks and countless mining pits, six or more feet deep, with accompanying gravel heaps, had to be skirted. One pit was only a few feet from the Clapp's cabin door.

In a later letter, Louise recorded:

"The first thing that attracted my attention as my new home came into view was the blended blue and white of the American banner, suspended on the Fourth of July last, by a patriotic sailor. He climbed to the top of the cedar tree to which he attached it, cutting away the branches as he descended, until it stood among its brethren, a beautiful moss-wreathed liberty pole, flinging to the face of Heaven the glad colors of the Free!"

Louise also pays particular attention to the artificial elegance of a hotel:

"Over the entrance is painted in red capitals the name of the great Humboldt, spelt with a d. This is the only hotel in the vicinity, and as there is a really excellent bowling alley attached to it, and the bar-room has a floor on which the miners can dance, and, above all, a cook who can play the violin, it is very popular. "But the clinking of glasses, and the swaggering air of some of the drinkers, reminds us that it is no place for a lady."

Louise Clapp liked doing things that others thought to be unladylike, such as mining for gold. When she washed a single pan of dirt, she found $3.25 in gold placer. She also discovered gold panning was hard, dirty work, and she did not repeat the experiment for years.

She did write about the gold miners, including the claiming system that governed the miners who owned the mines.

"First, let me explain to you the 'claiming' system," Louise Clapp wrote her sister Molly. "As there are no State laws upon the subject, each mining community is permitted to make its own.

"Here they have decided that no man may 'claim' an area of more than forty foot square. This he stakes off and puts a notice upon it. If he does not choose to work it immediately, he is obliged to renew the notice every ten days; for without this precaution, any other person has the right to 'jump it'.

"There are many ways of evading the above law. For instance, an individual can "holds' as many claims as he pleases if he keeps a man at work in each. The laborer can jump the claim of the man that employs him, but generally prefers to receive the six dollars per diem of which he is sure.

"The labor of excavation is extremely difficult on account of the immense rocks in the soil. Of course, no man can work out a claim alone. For that reason, they congregate in companies of four or six, generally designating themselves by the name of the place from whence the majority of the members have emigrated, for example, the 'Illinois', 'Bunker Hill', 'Bay State', etc. companies."

In Louise Clapp's third "Dame Shirley letter, she wrote of the setting of Rich Bar. She described it as a tiny valley, about eight hundred yards in length and 39 in width.

"It is hemmed in by lofty hills, almost perpendicular, draperied to thievery summits with beautiful fir trees, the blue blossomed Plumas and the Feather River undulating along their base.

"Here, the mining town sprang up suddenly, as if a fairy's wand had been waved above the bar. There were about forty tenements, round tents, square tents, plank hovels and log cabins. The residences varied in elegance and convenience from the palatial splendor of 'The Empire' down to a local habitation formed of pine boughs and covered with old calico shirts."

In her Dame Shirley Letters, Clapp described the people in the Rich Bar settlement.

"The people populating Rich Bar and Indian Bar varied as much as their houses. Besides white Americans and Californios (the Spanish-speaking residents), there were Swedes, Chilenos, Frenchmen, Mexicans, Indians, Hawaiians, Englishmen, Italians, Germans, American blacks and mulattos."

The blacks, she said, included Ned Paganini and trailblazer Jim Beckwourth. In her eighth Dame Shirley letter, she described Beckwourth:

"He is fifty years of age, and speaks several languages to perfection. As he has been a wanderer for many years and for a long time was a principal chief of the Crow Indians, his adventures are extremely interesting.

"He chills the blood of the green young miners, who, unacquainted with the arts of war and subjugation, congregate around him to hear the cold-blooded manner in which he relates the Indian fights that he has been engaged in.

"Unlike Jim Beckwourth, most men a Rich and Indian bars could not speak more than one language fluently, although some Americans seem to have tried. Nothing is more amusing than to observe the different styles in which Americans talk at the unfortunate Spaniard."

Mexicans in the mines were frustrated over the lack of justice. Louise Clapp addressed this issue in her 16th Dame Shirley letter.

"A few evenings ago, a Spaniard was stabbed by an American. It seems that the presumptuous foreigner had the impertinence to ask very humbly and meekly of that most noble representative of the stars and stripes, if the latter would pay him a few dollars which he owed him for some time.

"His high mightiness, the Yankee, was not going to put up with any such impertinence, and the poor Spaniard received, for answer, several inches of cold steel in his breast, which inflicted a very dangerous wound.

"Nothing was done and very little was said about this atrocious affair."

Dame Shirley's letter then explained that at Rich Bar a law was passed that no foreigner could work the mines on the Bar. This led to all the Spaniards to immigrate to Indian Bar.

Two years earlier, the California legislature passed a law requiring all foreigners to pay a $20 a month tax (later reduced to $4) for the right to stake a claim and mine it.

"On the Fourth of July, tensions between Californios and Americans exploded. While celebrating Independence Day with speeches, poetry, music and dancing at the Empire on Rich Bar, drunken celebrants made the rounds to Indian Bar.

When the Clapps returned to their cabin at Indian Bar, a man gave them an excited account of an American who had been knifed during a melee. Louise wrote about the incident in her 19th letter.

"A tall majestic-looking Spaniard, a perfect type of the novelist bandit of Old Spain, had stabbed Tom Somers, a young Irishman. Somers was a naturalized citizen of the United States.

"While brandishing the long knife with which he later inflicted the wound, he paraded unmolested down the street. When Tom Somers fell, the Americans being unarmed were seized with a sudden panic and fled.

"In a few moments, the Americans rallied and made a rush at the murderer, who immediately plunged into the river and swam to Missouri Bar. Eight or nine shots were fired at him, none hitting him.

"In the meanwhile, Spaniards thought the Americans had arisen against them. They barricaded themselves in a drinking saloon, determined to defend themselves against the massacre which was fully expected would follow.

"In the bake shop, which stands next to our cabin, Young Tom Somers lay straightened for the grave, while over his dead body a Spanish woman was weeping and moaning in the most piteous and heart-rending manner.

"The Rich Barians, who heard a most exaggerated account of the rising of the Spaniards against the Americans, armed with rifles, pistols, clubs, and dirks, were rushing down the hill by hundreds.

"Each one added fuel to his rage by crowding into the little bakery, to gaze upon the blood-bathed bosom of the victim. Then arose the most fearful shouts of 'Down with the Spaniards. Don't let one of the murderous devils remain'.

"The more sensible and sober of the Americans partly quieted the angry crowd. Fayette Clapp wanted his wife to join two other women who lived on a nearby hill where things would be safer should a serious fight erupt."

Louise said she wanted to stay where she was. Finally, like a dutiful wife, she joined the other ladies on the hill.

"We three women, left entirely alone, seated ourselves upon a log overlooking the strange scene below. The Bar was a sea of heads, bristling with guns, rifles and clubs. All at once, we were startled by the firing of a gun, and saw a man being led into the log cabin while another was carried, apparently lifeless, into a Spanish drinking saloon. A benevolent individual told us what had happened.

"It seems that an Englishman, the owner of the house of the vilest description, a person said to be the cause of all the violence of the day, attempted to force his way through the line of armed men.

"In his drunken fury, he tried to wrest a gun from one of them, which accidentally discharged in the struggle, inflicted a severe wound upon a Mr. Oxley and shattered in the most dreadful manner the thigh of Sr. Pizarro.

"This frightful accident recalled the people to their senses. They elected a vigilance committee and authorized persons to go arrest the suspected Spaniards.

"The first act of the "Committee was to try a Mejicana who had been foremost in the fray. She has always worn male attire, and on this occasion, armed with a pair of pistols, she fought like a very fury. Luckily, inexperienced in the use of fire arms, she injured no one. "She was sentenced to leave the Bar by daylight.

"The next day, the Committee tried five or six Spaniards. Two of them were sentenced to be whipped, the remainder to leave the Bar that evening, the property of all to be confiscated.

"Oh Mary! Imagine my anguish when I heard the first blow fall upon those wretched men. I had never thought that I should be compelled to hear such fearful sounds.

"One of these unhappy persons was a very gentlemanly young Spaniard who implored for death in the most moving terms. He appealed to his judges in the most eloquent manner—as gentlemen, as men of honor; representing to them to be deprived of life was nothing in comparison with the never-to-be effaced stain of the vilest convict's punishment to which they had sentenced him.

33

"Finding all his entreaties disregarded, he swore a most solemn oath, that he would murder every American that he should chance to meet alone, and as he is a man of the most dauntless courage, and rendered desperate by a burning sense of disgrace, he will doubtless keep his word."

It is believed by some that this flogging scene inspired a similar scene in John Rollin Ridge's book, *The Life and Adventures of Joaquin Murieta.*

Not long after this flogging incident, Louise Clapp reported a hanging and an attempted suicide at one of the mines. The first involved a man accused of murdering and robbing his employer.

The second case involved a man named Henry Cook, who had slit his own throat. After Dr. Clapp tended to his wound, Cook decided he would accuse the owner of the Humboldt of attempted murder. His accusation against the Humboldt owner was quickly dropped.

Irate citizens castigated Dr. Clapp for having bound the wound of a man who had raised his hand against his own life. The vigilantes decided to exile Cook from Rich Bar.

In her last letter to her sister Molly, Louise said they would be leaving the gold country because the gold was petering out and bad winter weather was expected. Still she expressed strong reservations.

"My heart is heavy at the thought of departing forever from this place. I like this wild and barbarous life; I leave it with regret. Yes, Molly, smile if you will at my folly; but I go from the mountains with a deep heart sorrow.

"I look kindly to this existence, which to you seems so sordid and mean. Here, at least, I have been contented. You would hardly recognize the feeble and half-dying invalid, who drooped so languidly out of sight, as night shut down between your straining gaze and the good ship *Manilla*."

In 1853, Fayette sailed to Hawaii without Louise. In 1854, he showed up in Massachusetts. A year later, he headed west again, this time to Illinois. Louise chose to remain in San Francisco, where she taught school.

She filed for divorce there in 1856. Although she kept Fayette's last name, she added an "e" to it, making her Louise A.K.S. Clappe. Fayette moved to Columbia, Mo., and remarried.

Her Dame Shirley Letters is still among the most sought-after history documents of the Gold Rush.

4

Lola Montez

Lola Montez

Lola Montez was christened Maria Dolores Eliza Rosanna Gilbert. She was the daughter of Ensign Edward Gilbert and his fourteen-year-old wife, who claimed descent from Spanish Nobility.

One of the first things one notices in the historical record of Lola Montez is the discrepancy in her birth date. Bruce Seymour, in his biography, *"Lola Montez, A Life"*, lists her date of birth as 1821.

Encylopedia Britannica shows her birth in Limerick, Ireland, as 1818. Whatever the real date, Lola Montez made headlines around the world.

Her father died in 1824 and her mother married Major John Craigie, later adjutant-general of the British army in India.

According to the Australian Dictionary of Biography, Lola, at age 19, was ordered by her mother to marry an aged judge. Lola, instead, eloped with Lieutenant Thomas James. They were married in Ireland July 23, 1839. James took his wife to Simla, India, where he eloped with another woman.

Under her given name, Marie Gilbert, Lola launched a career as a dancer. Her London debut as "Lola Montez" was disrupted when it was revealed that Lola was really Mrs. James.

If she had been less beautiful and less determined, this might have ended her career. She received additional dancing engagements throughout Europe.

Lola returned to England in 1842 and her husband James won a judicial separation on the grounds of Lola's adultery with the captain of the ship on which she was sailing.

Penniless, Lola fled to Europe, giving "suggestive performances" in Warsaw and Paris. She became the mistress of Franz Liszt, a Hungarian pianist and composer renowned in Europe during the "Romantic

Movement." She next became a consort of the French writer and dramatist Alexandre Dumas, and with Alexandre Dujarier, part owner of *LaPresse,* a French language daily newspaper.

After Dujarier was killed in a duel March 11, 1845, Lola went to Munich, posing as a Spanish noblewoman. The aging King Ludwig I of Bavaria became enamored of the beautiful Lola.

Ludwig bought her a large house and settled a sizable annuity on her. During her liaison with the King, Lola exerted considerable political influence for a time. According to Michael Cannon, writing in the Australian Dictionary of Biography, "Ministries rose and fell at her bidding and she won support from radical university students.

King Ludwig named her Countess Marie von Landsfeld. The Bavarian aristocracy refused to acknowledge her. Riots broke out in 1848 against her influence and thousands marched on the palace demanding her expulsion.

Lola fled to Switzerland when her Bavarian rights were annulled.

She returned to London in 1849 after going through the form of marriage to a young Guards officer, George Trafford Heald. She was arrested on August 6, 1849, on a charge of bigamy, but was released on bail.

She and Heald fled to Spain. Heald drowned the following year.

Lola returned to the stage, touring both Europe and America. She carried a cowhide whip and sometimes a pistol, and was often involved a assaults, scandals and legal actions.

This is a drawing of Lola Montez's house in Grass Valley. The letter sheet was mounted in the Jules Rupalley album, 1853-1857.

In San Francisco, Lola gave the first performance of her notorious *"Spider Dance"*. She soon went through another marriage performance, this time with Patrick Purdy Hull, owner of the *San Francisco Whig*. Hull soon sued for divorce, naming a German doctor as a co-respondent. A few days later, the doctor was found shot dead in the nearby hills.

In 1853, Lola Montez moved to Grass Valley, California, where she purchased a home. She hosted parties there, kept a pet bear and mentored the young Lotta Crabtree who lived on the same street.

The home has been remodeled and now houses the Nevada County Chamber of Commerce and a small Museum. It is listed as California Historical Landmark No. 292.

Lola appointed actor Noel Follin as her manager in May 1855. In June the couple sailed for Australia aboard the *Fanny Major*, with their own acting company.

In Sydney, they opened with a show entitled "Lola Montez in Bavaria". When Lola and Follin (who had changed his name to Folland) left Sydney two weeks later, they were followed by a sheriff's officer.

The officer carried a debtor's warrant of arrest. Lola undressed in her cabin and dared the officer to seize her. The officer left without her.

Lola opened at the Theatre Royal, Melbourne, opening with her Bavarian role. When audiences diminished, she began performing her *Spider Dance.*

She was denounced by the press for her performance. When she returned to Sydney in January 1856, she was met with packed houses. She enjoyed the same reception in Adelaide and at Ballarat.

When the *Ballarat Times* attacked her notoriety, Lola responded by horsewhipping the editor, Henry Seekamp, at the United States Hotel. Seekamp then published another unkind review and Lola sued him for criminal libel.

When the case came before the court, Lola failed to appear.

Besieged with syphilis, her body began wasting away. She died January 17, 1861 at age 42.

A quotation from James J. Ayers, in his reminiscences of Early California, 1922

"I took a position in the *Courier* office with Judge Crane. The assistant editor was "Pat" Hull, a good writer and very genial gentleman, who afterwards became the sixth, or ninth, or somewhere thereabouts, husband of that very eccentric woman, Lola Montez, the Countess of Landsfeldt.

"The Countess had built a cottage in 'Grass Valley', and was very fond of pets. Two of these were well-grown grizzly bears, which she kept chained at her front door.

"Poor Pat used to say, when speaking about his alliance with the famous Countess, that the greatest difficulty he encountered in his courtship was to get past those grizzly 'guardians of her palace gates.'

"But love laughs at grizzlies as well as locks, and 'Pat' won and married the lady. Then came the troubles. The most truculent of the bears, in a playful mood, breakfasted upon the calf of one of 'Pat's' legs, and he killed it.

"That was enough. War commenced in earnest between him and his spouse, and Lola carried her matrimonial grievances into court in the shape of a suit for divorce."

5

Eliza Marshall Gregson

(Author's note: Much of the following article was left unedited to retain the flavor of the story teller. Some miner corrections were made to make it more readable)

Eliza Marshall Gregson was a millworker and her husband, James Gregson was a blacksmith. The couple was married in Rhode Island in 1843 and started planning for a trip west.

In 1845, they set out for Oregon but joined a California wagon party along the way. When they arrived in California, John Sutter aided them and the Gregsons lived at his fort until 1847. Gregson then enlisted in the army under John C. Fremont.

When his war service ended, Sutter hired him to help James Marshall build a saw mill at Coloma. It was at this mill that James Marshall discovered gold, an event that started an epic migration to the west. While her husband was prospecting for gold in 1848 and 1849, Eliza bore and raised their children. Her duties didn't stop there.

To support the family, Eliza took in laundry and sewing jobs.

Eliza said she and her husband traveled to Coloma, he to help James Marshall build a saw mill, and she to cook for the fifteen men on Sutter's crew.

"The Indians that were about had never seen a white child. It was noised about that there was a white child on the place. The Indians came from 40 miles away to see my child."

"They would go so far as to pinch her shoulders and pull her hair to see if she was a real human. They were very fond of her. One squaw wanted me to swap babies with her."

Mrs. Gregson grew tired of not seeing any other white women. She was taken by wagon about 15 miles away to visit with a Mrs. Wimmer and her family.

"Well, I found her camping out and sleeping in the wagon. She was very glad to see me and we did not sleep very much but put in the time talking while I stayed there.

"She showed me a nugget of pure gold nearly as large as my thumb. William Scott, who had been camping with the Wimmer family found it in

January 1848. I stayed there two days and nights before returning to Coloma.

"About this time, there was a man named Turner came into Coloma with his daughter. I persuaded him to leave her with me while he went to bring the rest of his family. She was about 16-years old.

"I must say that for about three months our living was very poor. We had salt beef that looked like blue flint---& salt Salmon too salty & oily that it was not fit to eat and boiled barley and sometimes boiled wheat & peas. (We had) neither bread or Coffee or tea or sugar. We had 1 keg of Butter strong enough to run away with itself so that is the way we lived for three months.

"About this time gold hunters began to arrive with pans & in A short time the news began to spread far & wide about the first of May some men came up from Sonoma & told me that my little sister Mary Ann was married to a Doc. Ames an assistant Doc in the N.Y. Volunteers she being only a little past 13 years old.

"Somewhere about this time old James Marshall & J Gregson (her husband) went prospecting for gold a little further up the river than they had been and they found plenty of scale gold my husband asked Marshall to divide it with him.

"He very quickly answered no you are working for me. Very well says Gregson I will work no more & I shall gather gold for myself which he did.

"Now the people were coming in from all parts of Calif and Chili & by & by the Oregonians commenced arriving early in the gold excitement. Mr. Gregson made the first pick & afterwards made a good many picks and drills for the miners.

"The men stopt working on the mill. Everything was gold crazy. Runaway sailors and soldiers came to the hunt for gold. My sister's husband had deserted & she did not know where he was at that time."

6

Indian Peggy

Indian Peggy

Much of her history has been lost or clouded, but Indian Peggy is still honored as a heroine who saved Yreka from an Indian attack.

Her heroic act occurred in 1851 when relations between the Indians and the white men who rushed into the area to find gold were at their worst.

The miners began killing Indians who objected to the encroaching presence of the white men. The Indians maintained that the miners were invading and desecrating Indian tribal hunting grounds.

Relationships between the whites and the Indians deteriorated to a frightful situation. Indians became fearful and hostile towards the growing white population, who showed little regard for the environment in their search for the golden metal.

The Indians decided to rid their homeland of the white menace. The Indians formed a war party which would conduct a surprise attack on the gold camp of "Humbug City" and the town of Yreka.

Unlike many Indians, Indian Peggy had friends among both the white population and the Indian tribes. She sensed that an Indian attack on the gold camp and the town of Yreka would wreak havoc.

In 1852, Indian Peggy took it upon herself to prevent the almost certain massacre. Peggy lived on a nearby Rancheria. She walked the several miles to Humbug City and warned the people there to retreat to Yreka.

When the Indian war party arrived in Humbug City, it found the gold camp deserted. The Indians now knew they had lost the element of surprise and pulled back from their plans of attack, knowing they would become the target.

After her warning, Indian Peggy was invited to the town of Yreka to select anything she wanted, including blankets, warm clothing and food.

Indian Peggy lived to be at least 100 years of age. She died in 1902. Following her death, the Yreka High School closed to allow its students to attend her funeral.

Tyee Jim, Chief of the Shasta Nation, gave the eulogy, all in his native language.

7

Frances Cooper

"We came to California the same year as the ill-fated Donner Party," said France Cooper (now Mrs. Van Winkle. The Donner wagon train was about a month ahead of the Cooper wagon train, headed by Stephen Cooper, France's father.

"My father led his party of about eighty people across trackless plains and mountains for five months, simply with the sun and the stars as guides, and came west almost as straight as the crow flies.

"He believed in moving every day, if only three miles and the result was that all our oxen were in better condition when they arrived in California than when they started.

"Several of the survivors of the Donner party, young George Donner and Mrs. Reed, came to our house in Napa after they were rescued. I heard the other day that Mrs. Reed's daughter, 'Patty Reed, who was then a very little girl, is living on Franklin Street in Oakland. She is Mrs. Martha Lewis now.

"Both my father and mother were born in Kentucky, but like a good many other Kentuckians of those days, they moved out to Missouri, where we children were born.

"Then father was appointed Indian Agent at Council Bluffs, Iowa, old Colonel Thomas Benton getting him the position. There was no town there then—just the agency buildings.

"The only white people besides us were the blacksmith and another family. We children grew up with Indians as our playmates.

"There were several Indians—Chippewas, Ottawas and Pottawattomies—at the Council Bluffs agency when father was in charge. They were all lazy. They considered it a disgrace to work, and would rather be killed than made to labor.

"They didn't know any English, and wouldn't talk much in their own language, but as a girl I used to speak Indian.

"So, in May 1846, we started (to California), I then being 20 years of age. We hadn't been on the way a month—there were no roads or trails—when we were attacked by Indians.

"Five hundred Cherokees swooped down upon us on horseback and surrounded our wagon train. They rode around and around us. Father knew how to deal with Indians and after the wagons had been drawn together at the first alarm, he stepped out to parley with them, and offered them flour and tobacco.

"The Indians of those days were simply crazy for flour and tobacco. They would take a little flour, mix it with water and make it into tortillas and pat them lovingly for hours like little flapjacks and then cook them on hot stones.

"Father took out half a barrel of flour and measured it out, a little cupful to each Indian, and he cut a plug of tobacco up and gave it to them. Then they all smoked the pipe of peace. We knew father simply detested smoking; it made him sick, and we almost laughed to see him puffing away there with all those Indians.

"We ran into one herd of about 500 buffalo, and father killed several, but ordinarily he would not permit any delays or turning aside for game.

"There was no baggage but bedding and provisions. In one wagon, drawn by two big oxen we had the bedding, and we used to ride in that. We rode all the way except up the slopes of the Rocky Mountains and the Sierra Nevada.

"It was awful coming up those mountains. There were great rocks, waist high, that the wheels had to bump over, and it was all the poor oxen could do to drag the lightened loads.

"We were received at Napa by Mr. George Yount, who lived originally in Howard County, Missouri. He was just as glad to see us as if we had been his own family.

"He owned seven leagues of land there in the Napa Valley, had 600 mares and thousands of horses and cattle. The whole valley was covered with grazing cattle. In those days, the only Americans there were the Gregories, the Stewards, the Derbons and a few other families.

"There were so many thousands of long-horned Spanish cattle in the country that anybody that liked went out and killed a beef when he needed meat, and no one said anything. And it was good beef, too, probably because there was so much excellent grass.

"All the Spanish families had Indian slaves. They never permitted them to walk, but made them go about on the trot all the time. Those Indians made good slaves.

"The Spanish vaqueros used to ride in among the Indian Rancherias and drive out the boys and girls, leaving the mothers behind and killing the bucks if they offered any resistance. Then they would herd the captives down like so many cattle and sell them to the ranchers.

"About $100 was the standard price. A good girl would bring that, but some sold for as little as $50. I bought one Indian girl from a Spaniard for $100, but soon after that another Indian girl and two boys came to my house of their own accord and explained that they had no home and wanted to work.

The four of them did all my work, washing, ironing, cooking and housecleaning. One of the girls was a splendid nurse. The shameful treatment of the Indians by the Spanish was never equaled by the whites. As Americans settled up the country the enslaving of young Indians naturally stopped.

"We had a Fourth of July celebration given by us at the Yount place near Napa. There were about forty guests, most of them Spanish people of some prominence in the country.

"I made an enormous pound cake for the center of the table. Nobody had brought an American Flag to California, so my sister, now Mrs. Wolfskill of Winters, made a little one of some narrow red ribbon and cut some blue silk from her best dress, and sewed on one star, for material was very scarce. The whole thing was not bigger than a woman's handkerchief.

"We stuck it on top of the cake. One of our guests was Dr. Bailey, an Englishman of whom we thought a great deal. Father had written across the flag, 'California is ours as long as the stars remain.'

"We moved to Colusa. My husband owned half of Colusa and old Colonel Hagar owned the other half. We were the first white people in that part of the state.

"In the early days, we raised vegetables to sell to the miners, and we grew grain and shipped it down to San Francisco on steamers. When I first saw Sacramento it was an endless sweep of small tents, not a frame building anywhere in sight. That was in 1850. It was a terrifying place.

8

The Broken-Hearted Wife

A young man came to California, leaving behind a disconsolate wife who didn't agree with him heading to California and what would be a long separation.

After an arduous journey of five months, during which he experienced many hardships, he arrived safely in the gold country.

The man went readily to work in the mines but neglected to send any letters home. In a few months, he had dug a thousand dollars' worth of gold. Although he had not heard a word from home, he purchased a financial draft and sent the entire one thousand dollars to his wife.

However, the heart-broken wife had recovered her spirits and wondered why her husband had not contacted her. She decided if her husband had forgotten her, she would forget him.

She looked upon herself as an injured woman. She also looked upon another man to fill her husband's place. She applied for a bill of divorce which she easily obtained.

The very day after her second marriage, the draft for the one thousand dollars arrived from her first husband. But she could not touch a dollar of it.

It was sent to the order of Polly Smith. But alas, she was no longer Joe Smith's wife. She was Polly Brown, and Polly Brown couldn't endorse the draft.

9

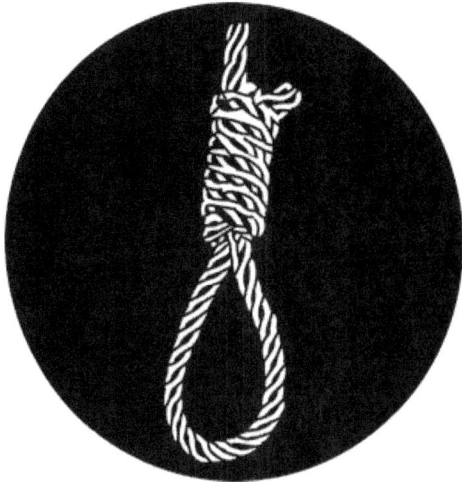

The Hanging of Juanita

It happened on such a festive day! It was the
Fourth of July when people were celebrating.
A young Mexican woman, variously called
Juanita and Josefa, was barely 20 years old. She sat
at one of the tables in Jack Craycroft's Gambling
Palace.

In one historical account, Juanita and her man,
Jose, who was a "monte" dealer in the Gambling
Palace, were giving their attention to a losing hand
of cards.

Frederick "Jock" Cannon, who has been described alternately as a Scotsman and as an Australian, was in a generous and drunken mood. In his drunkenness, he grabbed the bare shoulder of Juanita.

She retaliated by whipping out a knife from her garter and was out of her chair when Cannon's friends pulled him away. It was thought the incident was then put to rest.

Sometime later, in the wee hours of the morning, "Jock" Cannon, as he was known, and his friends were stumbling down the street, banging on doors. When they got to Juanita's house, they broke the door down.

The men later claimed they only knocked on the door and it fell down. While his friends say they pulled Cannon away, which ended the disagreement, Deputy Sheriff Mike Gray contends otherwise. He says they entered the house and created a disturbance.

This infuriated Juanita. (This information was never revealed at her trial).

It is said that Jock Cannon returned to her house later in the day. His friends say it was to apologize. Jose, however, demanded payment for the broken door.

An argument ensued and Juanita stepped between the men. Jock confronted her, calling her a whore. One account says he followed her into the house. When Jock was next seen he was stumbling out of the house. He had been stabbed in the heart and bled out on the ground.

A cry of murder went up throughout the little gold town of Downieville. Both Jose and Juanita were taken into custody and held in an empty building for trial.

Some reports say that care was taken to go through the proper procedure of an actual trial. Lawyers were appointed both for the prosecution and for the defense to present the case before a judge and a panel or jurors.

Cannon's friends gave their testimony concerning the breaking down of the door and the aftermath of the stabbing.

Jose stated that he heard Cannon call Juanita a whore and continue to use verbal abuse as he entered the house. Juanita said she was afraid of the men in town, including Jock Cannon, and was in the habit of sleeping with a knife under her pillow.

She admitted killing Cannon with the knife. She claimed she had rebuffed his sexual advances in the past. She testified that some Mexican boys had overheard some men discussing breaking into her house to have sex with her.

Her defense attorney, Cyrus D. Aiken testified that a doctor certified that Juanita was pregnant and that her innocent child should suffer the sins of the mother.

The angry mob demanded that other doctors examine her. These doctors disagreed with the pregnancy diagnosis. Defense Attorney Aiken was run out of town by the angry mob.

It is believed that racial tensions contributed to the crowd's anger at Juanita. Had she been a white woman, the hanging might have been postponed or even dismissed.

In this impromptu trial Juanita was sentenced to hang that very day. She was given one hour to prepare herself. Her boyfriend Jose was freed but encouraged to leave town.

While Juanita dressed for her hanging, a makeshift gallows was prepared on the bridge. When the time came, Juanita walked proudly in her finesse red hoop skirt. She also wore a Panama hat, which she tossed to Jose before the noose was placed around her neck.

When asked if she had anything to say, she said, "I would do the same thing again if I were treated as I have been."

Juanita died, hanging from the bridge on July 5, 1851. She won the dubious honor of being the first and only women hanging in California.

10

Jenny Cloud Wimmer

She tested James Marshall's
1848 Nugget in a Kettle of Lye Soap

Jenny considered herself just a cook. But being the gold camp's cook made her an important part of California's history.

Elizabeth Jane "Jennie" Cloud Wimmer was the daughter of Martin Cloud and Polly Cloud. Martin Cloud lost his prosperous tobacco operation because of an unscrupulous partner.

The Clouds moved to North Georgia from Virginia where Martin hoped to recoup his tobacco losses by making a fortune in prospecting for gold. In her spare time, Jennie traipsed the countryside panning for gold.

Little is known of her early life except that she married a young Georgia gold miner named Obadiah Baiz. The couple immigrated to Missouri to become farmers.

Jenny Wimmer

It was a journey that almost claimed Jenny's life. A log struck the plank ferry, causing it to capsize. Jenny was thrown into the churning muddy waters of the Mississippi. She grasped the tail of one of the oxen, clinging to the beast until it struggled ashore.

In Missouri, Jenny and Obadiah Baiz were neighbors with Peter and Polly Harlan Wimmer. Both Obadiah Baiz and Polly Wimmer died of a deadly malady called "wasting fever" (most probably cholera).

Jenny was left with two small children and Peter with five. Peter and Jenny were married the following year.

Captain George Harlan, the father of Peter's deceased wife Polly, was fascinated with California. He religiously read *Hastings Immigrant Guide to California.*"

In October 1845, he assembled a wagon train in Michigan, which traveled to Lexington, Missouri. The wagon train wintered there, waiting for warmer weather.

The wagon train broke camp the following spring. Peter and Jennie Wimmer and their brood of seven children were among the eighty-four immigrants going west.

After six months of travel, the immigrants arrived at Sutter's Fort on November 15, 1846, just days ahead of the ill-fated Donner-Reid Party which was stranded by a snowstorm in the Sierra Nevada.

Soon after arrival, Peter and his older sons went off to fight in the Mexican-American War. Jennie and the younger children were left at Sutter's Fort.

Peter was injured when a wagon loaded with cannon turned over on a rough road, forcing him to return to Sutter's Fort. John Sutter employed him to assist James Marshall in building a flour mill.

Before they could build a flour mill, Marshall and Wimmer had to find lumber, and that required building a saw mill. They located enough raw timber in Coloma.

Marshall hired a crew of thirteen Mormons and some local Indians. Peter Wimmer was put in charge of the Indians digging the mill race. Jennie Wimmer was employed as the camp cook.

Jennie was dismayed to find she was forced to cook over a crude, unvented open fire pit in their living quarters. When the weather permitted, she would cook over an open fire outside, but inclement weather forced her to cook inside in a smoke-filled room.

The mill hands eventually built a stone chimney for Jennie. But later, Jennie was confronted with a disagreement from the Mormon workers. They accused Jennie of saving the best portions of food for her own family.

Jennie countered, saying it was their own fault because they were always late for meals. When they did not respond on her first call on Christmas Day, she announced that she would not cook for them anymore.

Even though she later relented and cooked a fine meal that included meat, bread and both apple and pumpkin pies, one of the Mormons wrote a derogatory poem about Jennie. It was read aloud to the other mill workers.

> *"On Christmas morning in bed she swore*
> *That she would cook for us no more*
> *Unless we cum at the first call*
> *For I am Mistress of you all."*

Jennie was relieved when the Mormons built a new cabin for themselves and began doing their own cooking, especially since she was pregnant at the time. Benjamin Franklin Wimmer was born the following spring.

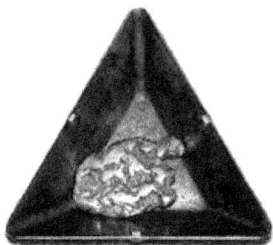

Wimmer Gold Nugget

When James Marshall made his discovery of gold in the mill race of the saw mill under construction, he wanted to make sure it was pure gold.

"It proved to be a nugget of gold"

There was a great deal of skepticism in the camp about the find. Many scoffed that it was only mica or fool's gold. Marshall and Peter Wimmer sent the nugget to Jennie to boil in a kettle of water.

In an interview with the San Francisco Bulletin in 1874, Jennie recalled recognizing it as gold. "I said this is gold, and I will throw it into my lye kettle, and if it is gold, it will be gold when it comes out."

It happened that Jennie was making soap on that very day. She knew that unlike mica or fool's gold, real gold would not be affected by being submerged in this pot of caustic potassium carbonate.

"I finished off my soap that day and set it out to cool. It stayed there until the next evening. At the breakfast table, one of the workman raised up his head from eating and said, 'I heard something about gold being discovered. What about it?'"

Marshall told him to ask Jennie and I told him it was in my soap kettle. A plank was brought in to lay my soap on. I cut it in chunks but the nugget was not to be found.

"At the bottom of the pot was a double handful of potash which I lifted in my two hands and right there was the gold piece, as bright as could be."

Ironically, it was one of the Wimmer children who "spilled the beans" about the gold find. He told a teamster about it who was delivering supplies to Coloma.

As soon as the teamster got back to Sacramento, he shared the news at Charlie Smith's store, and Smith in turn told his partner Sam Brannan who owned a newspaper in San Francisco.

James Marshall was plagued by gold seekers demanding that he help them strike it rich. His property was stolen, his cabin burned, and he had to flee for his life on two occasions.

The Wimmers left Coloma soon after gold was discovered, living in several locations in both northern and southern California. Peter died in San Luis Obispo County August 17, 1892.

The exact date of Jennie's death is not known, but is believed to have occurred soon after Peter's death. She is buried in a pioneer cemetery in San Diego County.

James Marshall gave her the nugget she tested as a keepsake. The nugget is now in the Bancroft Library at the University of California.

11

Eliza Donner Houghton

A Donner Party Survivor

Eliza Donner Houghton was the youngest daughter of George and Tamsen Donner. They were in the wagon train that became trapped at Donner Lake in the Sierra Nevada in 1846.

After several months, Eliza and her sisters were rescued by the third relief party to reach their camp. George and Tanner Donner both died in the mountains.

Eliza and her sister, Georgia, were taken in by Christian and Mary Brunner, elderly immigrants from Switzerland. In 1854, Eliza moved to Sacramento to live with her oldest half-sister, Elitha Donner Wilder, also a survivor of the Donner Party.

In 1861, Eliza married Sherman Otis Houghton, the widower of her cousin, Mary Donner, a party survivor. Eliza kept in contact with her fellow

Donner Party survivors and documented their stories.

Eliza Poor Donner Houghton

(Author's note": In this story, Eliza recounts the miserable conditions at Donner Lake in the winter of 1846-47)

"November ended with four days and nights of continuous snow and December rushed in with a wild, shrieking storm of wind, sleet, and rain, which ceased on the third.

"The weather remained clear and cold until the ninth, when Milton Elliot and Noah James came on snowshoes to Donner's camp, from the lake cabins, to ascertain if their captain was still alive, and to report the condition of the rest of the company.

70

George Donner, father of Eliza

"Before morning, another terrific storm came swirling and whistling down our snowy stairway, making fires unsafe, freezing every drop of water about the camp, and shutting us in from the light of heaven.

"Ten days later, Milton Elliott alone fought his way back to the lake camp with these tidings: 'Jacob Donner, Samuel Shoemaker, Joseph Rhinehart and James Smith are dead and the others in a low condition.

"Uncle Jacob, the first to die, was older than my father, and had been in miserable health for years before we left Illinois. He had gained surprisingly on the journey, yet quickly felt the influence of impending fate, foreshadowed by the first storm at camp. His courage failed. Complete prostration followed.

"My father and mother watched with him during the last night, and the following afternoon helped to lay his body in a cave dug in the mountainside, beneath the snow.

"That snow had scarcely resettled when Samuel Shoemaker's life ebbed away in happy delirium. He imagined himself a boy again in his father's house and thought his mother had built a fire and set before him the food of which he was fondest.

"But when Joseph Rhinehart's end drew near, his mind wandered, and his whitening lips confessed a part in Mr. Wolfinger's death; and my father, listening knew not how to comfort that troubled soul.

"He could not judge whether the self-condemning words were the promptings of a guilty conscience, or the ravings of an unbalanced mind.

"Like a tired child falling asleep, was James Smith's death; and Milton Elliot, who helped to bury the four victims and then carried the distressing report to the lake camp, little knew that he would soon be among those later called to render a final accounting. Yet, it was even so.

"Our camp having been depleted by death, Noah James, who had been one of my father's drivers, from Springfield until we passed out of the desert, now cast his lot with ours, and helped John 'Baptiste to dig for the carcasses of the cattle.

"It was weary work, for the snow was higher than the level of the guide marks, and at times they searched day after day and found no trace of hoof or horn. The little field mice that had crept into camp were caught then and used to ease the pangs of hunger.

"Also, pieces of beef hide were cut into strips, singed, and scraped, boiled to the consistency of glue, and swallowed with an effort; for no degree of hunger make the saltless, sticky substance palatable.

"Marrowless bones which had already been boiled and scraped were now burned and eaten, even the bark and twigs of pine were chewed in the vain effort to sooth the gnawing which made one cry for bread and meat.

"During the bitterest of weather we little ones were kept in bed, and my place was always in the middle where Frances and Georgia, snuggling up close, gave me of their warmth. From them I learned many things which I could never understand nor remember had they not made them plain.

"Just one happy play is impressed upon my mind. It must have been after the first storm, for the snow bank in front of the cabin door was not high enough to keep out a little sunbeam that stole down the steps and made a bright spot on the floor.

"I saw it and sat down under it, held it on my lap, passed my hand up and down in its brightness, and found that I could break its ray in two. In fact, we had quite a frolic.

"I fancied that it moved when I did, for it warmed the top of my head, kissed first one cheek, and then the other, and seemed to run up and down my arm. Finally, I gathered up a piece of it in my apron and ran to my mother.

"Great was the surprise when I carefully opened the folds and found that I had nothing to show, and the sunbeam I had left seemed shorter.

"After mother explained its nature, I watched it creep back slowly up the steps and disappear. Snowy Christmas brought us no 'glad tidings', and New Year's Day no happiness. Yet, each bright day that followed a storm was one of thanksgiving, on which we all crept up the flight of snow steps and huddled about on the surface in the blessed sunshine, but with our eyes closed against its painful and blinding glare.

"Once my mother took me to a hole where I saw smoke coming up, and she told me that its steps led down to Uncle Jacob's tent, and that we would go down there to see Aunt Betsy and my little cousins.

"I stooped low and peered into the dark depths. Then I called to my cousins to come to me, because I was afraid to go where they were. I had not seen them since the day we encamped.

"At that time they were chubby and playful, carrying water from the creek to their tent in small tin pails. Now, they were so changed in looks that I scarcely knew them, and they stared at me as if a stranger.

"So I was glad when my mother came up and took me back to our own tent, which seemed less dreary because I knew the things that were in it, and the faces about me.

"Father's hand became worse. The swelling and inflammation extending up his arm to the shoulder produced suffering which he could not conceal. Each day that we had a fire, I watched mother sitting by his side, with a basin of warm water upon her lap, laving the wounded and inflamed parts very tenderly, with a strip of frayed linen then wrapped around a little stick.

"I remember well the look of comfort that swept over his worn features as she laid the soothed arm back into place.

"By the middle of January, the snow measured twelve and fourteen feet in depth. Nothing could be seen of our abode except the coils of smoke that found their way up through the opening.

"There was a dearth of water. Prosser Creek was frozen over and covered with snow. Icicles hung from the branches of every tree. The stock of pine cones, that had been gathered to burn for light, was almost consumed.

"Wood was so scarce that we could not have fire enough to cook our strips of rawhide. Georgia heard my mother say that we children had not had a dry garment on in more than a week and she didn't know what to do about it.

"Then, like a smile from God, came another sunny day which not only warmed and dried us thoroughly but furnished a supply of water from dripping snowbanks.

"The twenty-first was also bright, and John Baptiste went on snowshoes with messages to the lake camp. He found the inmates in a more pitiable condition than we were. Only one death had occurred there since our last communication, but he saw several of the starving who could not survive many days.

"The number to consume the slender stock of food had been lessened, however, some six weeks previously, by the departure of William Eddy, Patrick Dolan, Lemuel Murphy, William Foster, Mrs. Sarah Fosdick, Mrs. William McCutchen, Mrs.

Harriet Pike, Miss Mary Graves, Franklin Graves, Sr., C.T. Stanton, Antonio, Lewis and Salvador.

"The party, which called itself 'The Forlorn Hope', had a most memorable experience. In some instances husband had parted from wife, and father from children. Three young mothers had left their babes in the arms of grandmothers. It was a dire resort, a last desperate attempt, in face of death, to save those dependent upon them.

"Staff in hand, they had set forth on snowshoes, each carrying a pack containing little save a quilt and light rations for six days' journeying. One had a rifle, ammunition, flint, and hatchet for camp use.

"William Murphy and Charles Burger, who had originally been of the number, gave out before the close of the first day and crept back to camp.

"The others continued under the leadership of the intrepid Eddy and brave Stanton. John Baptiste remained there a short time and returned to us saying, 'Those at the other camp believe the promised relief is close at hand.'

"This rekindled hope in us, even as it had revived courage and prolonged lives in the lake cabins, and we prayed, as they were praying, that the relief might come before it coming should be too late.

"Oh, how we watched, hour after hour, and how often each day John Baptiste climbed to the topmost bough of a tall pine tree and, with straining eyes, scanned the desolate expanse for one moving speck in the distance, for one ruffled track on the snow which should ease our awful suspense.

"Days passed. No food in camp except the unsavory beef hide—pinching hunger called for more. Again, John Baptiste and Noah James went forth in

76

anxious search for marks of our buried cattle. They made excavations, then forced their hand poles deep, deeper into the snow, but in vain their efforts—the nail and hook at the points brought up no sign of blood, hair or hide.

"It was a long weary waiting, on starvation rations until the nineteenth of February. I did not see any one coming that morning, but I remember there was an unusual air of excitement in the camp.

"Three strangers were there, and one was talking to father. The others took packs from their backs and measured out small quantities of flour and jerked beef and two small biscuits for each of us.

"Then they went up to fell the sheltering pine tree over our tent for fuel; while Noah James, Mrs. Wolfinger, my two half-sisters, and mother kept moving about hunting for things.

"Finally Elitha and Leanna came and kissed me, then father, "good-bye," and went up the steps out of sight. Mother stood on the snow where she could see all go forth.

"They moved in a single file—the leaders on snowshoes, the weak stepping in the tracks made by the strong. Leanna, the last in line, was scarcely able to keep up. It was not until after mother came back with Frances and Georgia that I was made to understand that this was the long-hoped for relief party.

"It had come and gone, and had taken Noah James, Mrs. Wolfinger, and my two half-sisters from us; then had stopped at Aunt Betsy's for William Hook, her eldest son, and my Cousin George, and all were now on the way to the lake cabins to join others who were able to walk over the snow without assistance.

"The rescuers, seven in number, who had followed instructions given them at the settlement, professed to have no knowledge of the Forlorn Hope, except that this first relief expedition had been outfitted by Captain Sutter and Alcalde Sinclair in response to Mr. Eddy's appeal.

"Other parties were being organized in California, and would soon come prepared to carry out the remaining children and helpless grown folk.

"By this, we knew that Mr. Eddy, at least, had succeeded in reaching the settlement."

12

Lotta Crabtree

Lotta Crabtree

Lotta was four years old when her father, in 1851, left his wife and daughter in New York to head for the California gold fields.

A year later, Mary Ann Livesey Crabtree closed the bookstore her husband had left behind to hunt for gold. With Lotta in tow, she booked passage on a steamship to San Francisco.

When Lotta and her mother arrived, her father, John Ashworth Crabtree, did not even meet them at the boat.

Mary Ann and Lotta befriended a group of entertainers, who gave them a temporary home. Mary Ann enrolled Lotta in dance classes.

After joining Lotta's father in Grass Valley, the Crabtrees ran a boarding house for gold miners. The tiny, red-haired Lotta danced and sang for the local miners. They showered her with gold nuggets and coins.

Lotta attracted the attention of a neighbor, dancer and actress Lola Montez. Montez encouraged her to keep entertaining. (*One story claims that Montez wanted to take Lotta on a tour of Australia, but her mother wouldn't allow it.*)

Lola's attention convinced Lotta's mother that her daughter had talent and signed her up for more lessons. The Crabtrees moved again and set up another boarding house, this one in Rabbit Creek, forty miles north of Grass Valley.

Here, Lotta made her first professional appearance at a tavern. She began touring throughout the California and Nevada gold country. She entertained miners by singing, dancing and playing the banjo.

Her mother, Mary Ann, continued as Lotta's stage manager. She would sweep the stage after every performance, looking for any bits of gold she might have missed.

Mary Ann was a shrewd businesswoman. When the leather bag became too heavy with gold, she bought real estate in the towns where Lotta toured.

Lotta pictured at the height of her career. She is said to sprinkle her hair with cayenne pepper to make it sparkle under stage lights.

The Crabtrees moved to San Francisco, where Lotta's demand grew, while also touring the

Sacramento and San Joaquin Valleys. The theatres in San Francisco brought Lotta to a real stage.

She at first experienced stage fright, but with encouragement and coaxing of Mary Ann she became a professional. By 1859, she was, *Miss Lotta, the San Francisco Favorite.*

At age 16, Lotta performed a farewell show in San Francisco. The Crabtrees sailed back to New York, where Lotta acted in plays such as *Uncle Tom's Cabin*, and *Little Nell and the Marchioness*, adapted for her by John Brougham from Charles Dickens' *The Old Curiosity Shop.*

By age 20, Lotta was a national star. By 1875, she was touring with her own company, rather than using local stock companies.

Lotta had many admirers but she never married. She said her mother would never allow it because it would end her ability to be considered forever young. By the 1880s, Lotta was the highest paid actress in America. She earned up to $5,000 per week for her performances.

While traveling abroad with Mary Ann and her brothers, Lotta learned to speak French. She visited museums and took up painting, which she pursued for the rest of her life.

In 1885, Mary Ann purchased a choice parcel at a resort on the shores of Lake Hopatcong, New Jersey. She contracted with noted architect Frank Furness to design a summer cottage.

This cottage was hardly a cottage at all. It was an eighteen room mansion with a wine cellar, a billiard room, music room, library, beautiful fireplaces and sweeping verandas.

Lotta suffered injuries in a bad fall at Wilmington, Delaware in 1889. She attempted a comeback in 1891, but then retired permanently from the stage in 1892. She was 45 years old.

She and her mother retreated to the summer cottage at Lake Hopatcong. When her mother died in 1905, Lotta sold the lake house and became reclusive.

Lotta made one final appearance in 1915 for Lotta Crabtree Day in San Francisco. She then purchased the Brewster Hotel in Boston, where she lived alone.

13

Catherine Haun

Catherine Haun was the wife of a middle-class lawyer in Iowa when they heard the news of the California Gold Rush. Although pioneering was usually initiated by men, they were by no means the only ones engaged in that endeavor.

Many single men—and married men acting as temporary bachelors—seduced by the thought of rich lands and lodes, traveled west; but settlement was often contingent on the possibility of making and enduring families there.

Thousands of women, therefore, trudged the Overland Trail after 1840 when the great westward migration took off. Most of the women were married. While some of them were forced to make the move, many other insisted on accompanying their men.

"Early in January we first thought of immigrating to California. It was during hard times, and as we were financially engaged in our business interests in Clinton, Iowa. We longed to go to the new El Dorado and pick up gold enough with which to return and pay off our debts.

"Gold fever was contagious and few, old or young, escaped the malady. On the streets, in the fields, in the workshops and by the fireside, golden California was the chief topic of conversation.

"Some half-dozen families of our neighborhood joined us making about twenty-five persons in our little band.

"On April 24, 1849, we left our comfortable homes—and uncomfortable creditors—for the uncertain and dangerous trip. There was still snow on the ground and the roads were bad.

"Our trunk of wearing apparel consisted of 'bare-back' underclothing, a couple of blue checked gingham dresses and several large stout aprons for general wear. Also included were a pink calico sunbonnet and a white one for dress-up days.

"I wore a dark woolen dress which served me almost constantly throughout the whole trip. The wool protected me from the sun's rays and penetrating prairie winds.

"The canvas-covered schooners were supposed to be constructed upon the principle of the 'wonderful one-horse shay'. It was essential to have animals be sturdy, whether oxen, mules or horses. Oxen were preferred as they were less likely to stampede or be stolen by Indians. In an emergency, they could be used as beef.

"We decided to draw up a code of regulations for wagon train government and mutual protection. John Brophy was selected as Colonel. He was particularly eligible having served in the Black

Hawk War and his experience with Indians was exceptional.

"Each week seven Captains were appointed to serve on Grand Duty. They were to protect the camps and animals at night. In case of danger they were to give the alarm.

"When the campground was desirable enough to warrant it we did not travel on the Sabbath. The men used this day to repair wagons, harness, yokes and shoeing the animals. The women washed clothes, boiled a big mess of beans to be used over several meals, or mended clothes.

"Indians were a source of anxiety during the entire trip. 'We were never sure of their friendship. "On the barren plain, we carried empty bags and each pedestrian picked up buffalo chips to be used as fuel.

"One man was bitten on the ankle by a venomous snake. Although ever available remedy was tried, his leg had to be amputated with a common handsaw. Fortunately for him, he had a brave wife who helped and cheered him along.

"It was not long before he found much that he could do and was not considered a burden. He was of a mechanical turn, and later on helped repair wagons, yokes and harness.

"When the train was on the move, he sat in the wagon, gun by his side, and repaired shoes and boots. He was one of the most cheery members of the company and told good stories and sang at the campfire.

"We had not traveled many miles in the Black Hills—the beginning of the Rocky Mountains—before we realized our loads would have to be lightened.

The animals couldn't draw the heavily-laden wagons over the slippery roads.

"We were obliged to sacrifice most of our merchandize that was intended to be our stock in trade in California. We left it by the wayside.

"It was the Fourth of July when we reached the beautiful Laramie River. Its sparkling pure waters were full of fish that could be caught with scarcely any effort.

Laramie River had sparkling pure water.

"Cholera was prevalent on the plains. The train preceding us, as well as the one following ours, had one or more deaths. We fortunately did not have a single case of the disease. The Indians spread the disease by digging up the bodies of the victims for their clothing.

"It was with considerable apprehension that we started across the treeless, alkali region of the Great Basin or Sink of the Humboldt. Our wagons were badly worn, the animals much the worse for wear, food and stock feed was getting low with no chance of replenishing the supply.

"We reached Sacramento on November 4, 1849, just six months and ten days after leaving Clinton, Iowa. For Christmas dinner, we had a grizzly bear steak for which we paid $2.50, one cabbage for $1.00 and—oh horrors—some more dried apples.

The town of Sacramento in 1849.

"For a Christmas present, the Sacramento River rose very high and flooded the whole town.

"It was past the middle of January before we reached Marysville—there were only a half-dozen houses, all occupied at exorbitant prices. Someone was calling for the services of a lawyer to draw up a will and my husband offered to do it for which he charged $150.

"This seemed a happy omen for success and he hung out his shingle, abandoning all thought of going to the mines. We were happy to settle down and begin housekeeping in a shed that was built in a day with lumber purchased from that first lawyer fee."

14

Juliette Brier

Juliette Brier

In October 1849, a group of travelers gathered in Provo, Utah on their way to the California gold fields. Most of them came south to Utah to avoid the winter snows in the Sierra Nevada.

Juliette Brier was a part of that group. She was described as a wisp of a woman, nervous by nature and the mother of three sons, aged eight, seven and four.

Everyone in the group came to feel that Juliette was "the best man in the whole wagon train".

It was Juliette that put the packs on the oxen in the mornings, took them off at night. She lighted the fires, cooked the food, helped with the children and nursed her husband through dysentery.

Juliette simply did everything, when her husband claimed to be too tired. "This," said one member of the party, "seemed to be most of the time."

When her party started out for Los Angeles on October 9, 1849, there were 80 wagons and two-hundred and fifty people. There were one thousand head of horses and cattle.

The guide for the immense wagon train was Jefferson Hunt, a member of the Mormon Battalion. Hunt was on his way via the Old Spanish Trail to Los Angeles to buy supplies for the Salt Lake community.

He organized the wagon train into seven divisions, each with its own captain. The wagon train company named itself, "The Sand Walking Company".

Early in their journey Hunt took a wrong turn. Although he corrected it, the travelers lost confidence in him.

Captain Smith, who was leading a pack train party of nine Mormons, rode up with a map showing a cutoff from the trail over Walker Pass. It looked tantalizing to many in the wagon train.

There was a great deal of argument, but finally, the Briers and four other families, the Bennetts, the Arcanes, the Wades, and the Dales chose to go with the short cut.

Captain Hunt warned them they might be walking into the "jaws of hell". Juliette's husband, the Reverend John Wells Brier, stubborn and eager to strike it rich, urged others to join him in setting out on their own.

On November 7, after three days of following the bogus map, Brier's wagon spotted mountains ahead. Seventy-two of the wagons backtracked to rejoin Hunt's crew.

Seven week later, that group arrived in Los Angeles without mishap.

But for the remaining 27 wagons, including the Brier, Wade, Bennett and Arcane families, it was to be a nightmare journey.

As far as the eye could see, there was nothing living in the desert. It was a wind-blown and sunbaked waste, with the aptly named Funeral Range in the center.

A few days into the journey, they ran short of water. When her husband went ahead to look for water, Juliette was left alone to not only care for her children, but to help with the wagon and the thirsty cattle.

When darkness fell, she lost sight of the two others in her group. She crawled on her knees with her youngest son, Kirk on her back to find the ox tracks in the starlight.

It was 3 a.m. before she found the others, along with her husband, camped at a hot and cold springs. They named it "Furnace Creek".

When morning came, someone suggested that Juliette should remain at the creek. Her reply was simple: "I have never kept the company waiting, neither have my children. Every step I take will be towards California."

One time, one of her oxen sunk chest deep in mud. She went in after it. Juliette refused to abandon the beast. Finally another member of the party came to help her. Her husband sat idly by.

A fellow pioneer described his conduct as that of an "invalid preacher who had never earned his bread by the sweat of his brow."

The next morning, they caught up with another wagon party, the Jayhawkers, who were burning their wagons in order to make travelling through the desert easier.

The Briers abandoned their wagon. While Juliette strapped her diminishing rations onto their failing oxen, Rev. Briers asked for permission to travel with the Jayhawkers.

Twenty miles into the desert, the travelers' tongues were swollen and their lips cracked. Some of the oxen lay down to die. Some of the men took to climbing the rock-strewn mountains to bring back snow in their shirts to supplant the shortage of water.

Meals often consisted of bones boiled in ox blood. Dehydration and hunger took over. Juliette's weight dropped to a mere 75 pounds or less.

On New Year's Day, they camped at the head of the Panamint Valley, totally lost.

Finally, after herding their oxen, the Brier family emerged from purgatory.

Juliet Brier earned the Jayhawkers respect and affection, one recalling that in walking nearly one hundred miles through sand and sharp-edged rocks, she frequently carried her children on her back, another in her arms and held a third by the hand.

At Jayhawker reunions, Juliette Brier was honored as being the first white women to enter Death Valley.

15

Eliza Farnham

Eliza Farnham became steeped in women's rights issues at an early age. When her mother died, five-year-old Eliza was separated from her father and siblings. She was placed in the home of the Warrens, a childless couple.

She was forced to work as a servant for the Warrens, who she said in later years were Quakers, "yet thoroughly atheistic". The only reading materials in the house were condemnations of religion and praise of reason, including Paine and Voltaire.

Elizabeth Farnham

Maggie MacLean published a clearly defined paper on the life, accomplishments and failures of Eliza Farnham. Eliza was largely self-educated, she found solace in books and in nature.

After seven years under the Warren's stringent working conditions, Eliza contacted a brother to bring her out of the wilderness. At age 15, Eliza went to live with an aunt and uncle and briefly attended the Albany Female Academy. Her aunt, Eliza later wrote, "raised her through neglect and hardship."

Eliza stole money from her aunt, convinced that it was owed her as compensation for her labor and the unfulfilled obligation to educate her.

Over the next 10 years, Eliza became self-educated, civilized and superficially Christianized.

In 1836, Eliza married lawyer and author Thomas Jefferson Farnham, who was ten years her senior. Farnham organized and took command of an ill-fated invasion to drive the British out of the Willamette Valley of Oregon.

He then turned to central California as a more promising site for his expansionist ambitions. In Santa Cruz he joined the Yankee community and acquired land from a Californio family in payment for his services.

Meanwhile, Eliza moved to New York. Still looking for paying work, Eliza took a job as Women's Warden of the infamous Sing Sing Prison. She won the appointment through her favorable connections with Horace Greeley and other reformers.

Farnham adopted modern notions of rehabilitation to women prisoners, who were formerly regarded as irredeemable. She instituted, emphasizing kind treatment, the use of music, and other improvements in the living environment at Sing Sing.

Prison trustees came to view her as a dangerous radical, and in 1848, they succeeded in driving her out.

While working as a teacher in Boston, Eliza learned that her husband Thomas, with whom she had lived only briefly, died in California. He left her some real estate. This occurred when the discovery of gold in California was drawing hordes of prospectors on every ship.

Eliza made plans to go west to settle her husband's estate. To finance the trip, she conceived a plan to take a boatload of good women to "civilize" California.

While the project gained the endorsement of several reformers, the project itself, failed. Eliza and her two son sons sailed for California in May 1849 with one other woman, a Miss Sampson, and her nursemaid.

Along the way, the nursemaid ran off with a crew member. When the ship stopped at Valparaiso, Farnham went in search of a replacement nursemaid for Miss Sampson.

The Captain departed without her before she returned to the ship, taking the rest of her goods, including her two sons, with the steamship.

Farnham waited in Chile for almost two months for the next ship. When she arrived in San Francisco, she found one of her sons was quite ill. With both her children and her baggage, Eliza made her way to Santa Cruz where her inherited land was located.

She took possession of the 200-acre ranch, naming it El Rancho La Libertad.

Eliza focused her initial housekeeping efforts on getting a stove installed. She called the next three days, "the siege of the stove". A hired man failed in the effort, as did her friend Miss Sampson. In the end, Eliza Farnham, herself, tackled the job.

She described her "casa" at Santa Cruz "as not a cheerful specimen". Not afraid of labor, Farnham set to building a house.

"My first participation in the labor of its erection was the tenanting of the joists and studding for the lower story, a work in which I succeeded so well, that during its progress I laughed, when I paused for a few moments rest, at the idea of promising to pay a man $14 to $16 per day for doing what I found my own hands so dexterous in.

Eliza's friend and employee at Sing Sing, Georgiana Bruce, joined her and her sons in Santa Cruz. The women roofed and joined the new house, broke sod and set out potatoes, planted fruit trees and raised poultry.

To their neighbors' amusement, the women wore bloomer costumes which allowed them to work and move freely.

In California, Eliza Farnham farmed the land, taught elementary school, worked on her writing, and became a leading abolitionist, author and feminist.

In the mid 1850's, she embarked on a series of well-attended lectures throughout Northern California. She promoted her views on Spiritualism, women's health issues and other social concerns.

Eliza closely observed the local society of Santa Cruz. As she saw it, it was in desperate need of women's moral influence. California's population was more than 90 percent male at the time.

Farnham believed that women neither needed nor would benefit from individual legal and political rights, because women were already superior to men.

In 1852, Eliza married William Fitzpatrick. Maggie MacLean wrote: "Although she preached marriage as the highest service a woman could render to the new state of California, her own marriage was brief and abusive.

In 1856, Eliza obtained one of the first recorded divorces in California and left the state.

She returned to California to serve as matron of the state's first mental hospital, the Stockton Insane Asylum, from 1859 to 1862.

Farnham became ill with tuberculosis in 1864. She died December 15, 1864 at age 49.

16

Jessie Benton Fremont

When Jessie and John Charles Fremont, a young officer in the Topographical Corps, began dating, her parents, Senator Thomas Hart Benton and his wife Elizabeth forbade them from seeing each other.

Against her father's wishes, the couple secretly married. Senator Benton chose to make the best of it and used his considerable influence to further his son-law's career as an explorer.

In the spring of 1842, Fremont left his now-pregnant Jessie to lead his first expedition to mark the trails of the west. He returned just days before the birth of Elizabeth Benton (known as Lily).

While her husband was on his first expedition, Jessie served as Senator Benton's hostess and occasionally translated secret Spanish documents for the State Department.

Jessie Ann Benton Fremont

As her husband prepared to leave on his second expedition, Jessie intercepted and suppressed an order from Washington, D.C. that she feared threatened his command.

She urged John to leave at once, and then wrote to authorities in Washington explaining what she had done.

Jessie took an intense interest in the details of her husband's expedition. She became his recorder, making notes as Fremont described his experiences and them writing them out.

She not only wrote them out, but added human-interest touches that made the printed reports best-sellers. This became her life's work, interpreting her husband's actions for an eager public.

Jessie and John Charles Fremont

While Fremont defended his actions in the Bear Flag Revolt in a military trial, Jessie gave birth to a second child, Benton. She blamed the baby's death on General Stephen Kearney, who brought the action against Fremont.

In 1849, Jessie traveled over the Isthmus of Panama with her six-year-old daughter to meet her husband. The Fremont's son, John Charles, was born at their ranch in California, "Las Mariposa".

The Fremont's grew wealthy. When her husband ran for President of the U.S. in 1855, (he was defeated by James Buchanan), Jessie took what little part custom allowed in his campaign.

After his defeat, the Fremont's moved back to Black Point, overlooking the Golden Gate in San Francisco.

The State of Missouri took possession of the Pacific Railroad in February 1866 when the company defaulted on its interest payment. The railroad was sold in a private sale to John Fremont.

Jessie Fremont in her later years.

Fremont reorganized the assets of the Pacific Railroad as the Southwest Pacific Railroad. In less than a year, the railroad was repossessed by the state of Missouri when Fremont was unable to pay the second installment on his purchase.

In 1878, President Hayes appointed Fremont as the 5th Territorial Governor of Arizona. Jessie, with her daughter Lily, her son, Frank, her Irish maid Mary, her cook Ah Chung, and a dog named Thor, arrived in Prescott, Arizona.

Jessie stayed only one year, citing the high altitude and health reason, she moved back to New York.

Now destitute, the family depended on the publication earnings of Jessie.

When Jessie learned of her husband's death July 28, 1890, in New York City, she and Lily were in Los Angeles. They moved into a home built for them in

Los Angeles by a committee of California women. Jessie died there December 27, 1902.

Jessie was buried with her husband on the banks of the Hudson River in New York.

Nancy Kelsey

Nancy Kelsey

"Where my husband goes, I can go. I can better endure the hardships of the journey than the anxiety from an absent husband."

Nancy Kelsey married her husband Ben in Missouri, where he and his brothers, David, Samuel and Andrew settled a section of land in St. Clair County.

The brothers, including Ben, were in trouble with authorities, accused of some shady dealings in a real estate transaction. Samuel was indicted for murder and a lawsuit was filed against Andrew in 1841.

Nancy Kelsey was 17 years old when Ben decided to travel west. Their second child, named after Samuel, died after living only eight days.

Shortly after, Ben and Nancy and their one-year-old daughter, along with Ben's brothers, joined John Bidwell's first wagon train to California.

Nancy's sister, Betsey Grey, was married to Richard Phelan along the trail to California.

One emigrant group, including Nancy's sister Betsey and her husband, went directly to Oregon. The other group, including Nancy, daughter Martha Ann and Ben Kelsey, took the route through Utah, as detailed in a letter written by Dr. John Marsh. Marsh had never seen the route he described in the letter.

Nancy described their trip in an interview with the *San Francisco Examiner*. In the interview, Nancy said, "The group had no guide and no compass." On September 16, the wagons and most of their contents were left on the west face of Nevada's Ruby Mountains, near Owens Lake and present-day Oasis, Nevada.

The party then proceeded on foot with pack horses. According to Nancy's interview with the San Francisco Examiner, the party was attacked a number of times and had their provisions and horses stolen.

"We left our wagons and finished our journey on horseback and drove our cattle. I carried my baby in front of me on the horse. At one place the Indians surrounded us, armed with their bows and arrows. My husband

leveled his gun at the chief and made him order his Indians out of arrow range."

On September 24 they found the Mary River that was listed in Marsh's description. It is now called the Humboldt River located at the base of the Sierra Nevada mountain range.

The 34 members arrived in California via the Sonora Pass and followed the Stanislaus River downhill. They reached the confluence with the San Joaquin River November 3.

Several members of the group, including the Kelseys, stopped at Dr. Marsh's ranch at the foot of Mount Diablo.

During 1842, Nancy and Ben Kelsey worked for John Sutter collecting elk hides at Clear Lake. They left Sutter's employ in 1843 and drove cattle north along the California-Oregon Trail. Nancy was pregnant.

In Oregon, Nancy delivered Sarah Jane Kelsey, who died eight days later. Nancy became pregnant again right away and delivered daughter Margaret in 1843.

After selling their cattle, the Kelseys returned to California, settling on 2,000 acres in Calistoga, California. They were neighbors of General Vallejo's property to the south.

During the Bear Flag Rebellion in 1846, the Kelsey brothers joined John C. Freemont in declaring California's independence from Mexico. Nancy Kelsey, Mrs. John Sears, and Mrs. Benjamin Dewell sewed the original Bear Flag from a pattern drawn by William L. Todd, a nephew of Mary Todd Lincoln.

Original Bear Flag sewn by Nancy Kelsey, Mrs. John Sears and Mrs. Benjamin Dewell.

The words "California Republic" were inked in pokeberry juice, the fabrics were borrowed from what little was available, and many said the bear looked more like a pig. Fortunately, it had to serve only 24 days until the U.S. Navy claimed California for the United States.

Major General John Charles Fremont and Ben Kelsey became enemies when Fremont ordered Kelsey to kill Jose de los Reyes Berryessa, a Mexican neighbor and the twin sons of Francisco de Haro.

Kelsey refused. They were killed by Fremont's scout Kit Carson.

In 1848, Ben took fifty Pomo Indians from his brother Andrew's ranch to mine for gold. They established a mining camp called Kelsey Diggings in the Sierra foothills near Sutter's Mill.

Once at the diggings, Ben sold all of the company's supplies to other miners and returned home to Sonoma, ill with malaria. While sick, he shot a Native American dead for accosting Nancy, who had ridden into town to get Ben some medicine.

17

Mary Ballou

(Author's Note: No editor could say what Mary Ballou had to say as well as her poignant letter says it, spelling and grammar aside. No attempt was made to correct the grammar or punctuation in this letter. The only editing of the letter was to break it into paragraphs to make it more readable. Mary Ballou, who ran a boarding house during the California Gold Rush, described her living accommodations in a letter to her son, Selden, in 1852.)

"All the kitchen that I have is four posts stuck down into the ground and covered over the top with factory cloth no floor but the ground. this is a Boarding House kitchen. There is a floor in the dining room and my sleeping room covered with nothing but cloth. We are working in a Boarding House.

"Oct 27 this morning I awoke and it rained in torrents, well I got up and I thought of my House. I went and looket into my kitchen, the mud and water was over my Shoes I could not go into the kichen to do any work to day but keep perfectly dry in the Dining so I got along very well. Your Father put on his Boots and done the work in the kitchen. I felt badly to think that I was de(s)tine to be in such a place. I wept for a while and then I commenced singing and made up a song as I went.

"now I will try to tell you what my work is in this Board House. well, sometimes I am washing and Ironing sometimes I am making mince pie and Apple pie and squash pies. Sometimes frying mince turnovers and Donuts.

"I make biscuit and sometimes Indian jonny cake and then again I am making minute puding filled with rasons and Indian Bake puddings and then again a nice Plum Puding and then again I am Stuffing a Ham of pork that cost forty cents a pound.

"Sometimes I am making gruel for the sick, now and then cooking oisters sometimes making coffee for the French people strong enough for any man to walk on that has Faith as Peter had.

"three times a day I set my Table which is about thirty feet in length and do all the little fixings about it such as filling pepper boxes and vinegar cruits and mustard pots and Butter cups.

"sometimes I am feeding my chickens and then again I am scareing the Hogs out of my kitchen and Driving the mules out of my Dining room. you can see by the descrption of that I have given you of my kitchen that anything can walk into the kitchen and then from kitchen to the Dining room so you see the

Hogs and mules can walk in any time day or night if they choose to do so.

sometimes I am up all times a night scaring the Hogs and mules out of the House. last night there a large rat came down pounce down onto our bed in the night. Sometimes I take my fan and try to fan myself but I work so hard that my Arms pain me so severely that I kneed some one to fan me so I do not find much comfort anywhere.

"I made a Bluberry puding to day for Dinner. Sometimes I am making soaps and cramberry tarts and Baking chicken that cost four Dollars a head and cooking Eggs at three Dollars a Dozen. Sometimes boiling cabbage and Turnips and frying fritters and Broiling stake and cooking codfish and potatoes. I often cook nice Salmon trout that weigh from ten to twenty pounds apiece.

"sometimes I am taking care of Babies and nursing at the rate of Fifty Dollars a week but I would not advise any Lady to come out her and suffer the toil and fatigue that I have suffered for the sake of a little gold neither do I advise any one to come.

"Clarks Simmon wife says if she was safe in the States she would not care if she had not one cent. She came in here last night and said, 'Oh dear I am so homesick that I must die,' and then again my other associate came in with tears in her yes and said that she had cried all day.

Mary Ballou's simple headstone.

"she said if she had as good a home as I had got she would not stay twenty minutes in California. I told her that she could not pick up her duds in that time. she said she would not stop for duds nor anything else but my own heart was two sad to cheer them much.

(Editor's note: The reference to "in the States" indicated how far from home the gold miners felt because California was not a state at this time)

"now I will tell you a little more about my cooking. Sometimes I am cooking rabbits and Birds that are called quails here and I cook squrrels. occasionly I run in and have a chat with Jane and Mrs. Durphy and I often have a hearty cry. no one but my maker knows my feelings. and then I run into my little cellar which is about four feet square as I have no other place to run that is cool.

"October 21 well I have been to church to hear a Methodist sermon. his text was let us lay aside every weight and the sin that doth so easely beset us. I was the only Lady that was present and about forty gentlemen. So you see that I go to church when I can.

"November 2 well it has been Lexion here to day. I have heard of struggling and tite pulling but never

118

saw such aday as I have witnessed to day the Ballot Box was so near to me that I could hear every word that was spoken.

"the wind blows very hard here tto day. I have three lights Burning and the wind blows so hard that it almost puts my lights out while I am trying to write. If you could but step in and see the inconvience that I have for writing you would not wonder that I cannot write any better you would wonder that I could write at all.

"notwithstanding all the dificuty in writing I improve every leishure moment. it is quite cool here my fingers are so cold that I can hardly hold my pen.

"well it is ten o'clock at night while I am writing. the people have been Declareing the votes. I hear them say Hura for the Whigs and sing whigs songs. now I hear them say that Morman Island has gone whig and now another time a cheering, now I hear them say Beals Bar has gone whig now another time of cheering. well it is getting late and I must retire soon there is so much noise I do not expect to sleep much to night. there has been a little fighting here to day and one challenge given but the chalenge given but the chalenge given was not accepted they got together and setted their trouble.

"I will tell you a little of my bad feelings, on the 9 of September there was a little fight took place in the store. I saw them strike each other though the window in the store. One went and got a pistol and started towards the other man.

"I never go into the store but your mothers tender heart could not stand that so I ran into the store and Beged and plead with him not to kill him for eight or ten minutes not to take his Life for the sake of his wife and three little children to spare his life and then I ran through the Dining room into my sleeping room and Buried my Face in my bed so as not to hear the sound of the pistol and wept Biterly.

"Oh I thought if I had wings how quick I would fly to the States. that night at the supper table he told the Boarders if it had not been for what that Lady said to him Scheles would have been a dead man. after he got his pashion over he said that he was glad that he did not kill him so you see that your mother has saved one Human beings Life, you see that I am trying to relieve all the suffering and trying to do all the good that I can.

"there I hear the Hogs in my kichen turning the Pots and kettles upside down so I must drop my pen and run and drive them out. so you see this is the way that I have to write—jump up every five minutes for something and then again I washed out about a Dollars worth of gold dust the fourth of July in the cradle so you see that I am doing a little mining in this gold region but I think it harder to rock the cradle to wash out gold than it is to rock the cradle for Babies in the states.

"October 11 I washed in the forenoon and made a Democrat Flag in the afternoon sewed twenty yards of splendid worsted fringe around it and I made whig flag. I had twelve Dollars for making them so you see that I am making Flags with all rest of the various kinds of work that I am doing and then again I am scouring candlesticks and washing floor and making soft soap. The people tell me that it is the first Soft Soap they knew made in California.

"Sometimes I am making mattresses and sheets. I have no windows in my room. all the light that I have shines through a canvas that covers the House and my eyes are so dim that I can hardly see to make a mark so I think you will excuse me for not writing any better. I have three Lights burning now but I am so tired and Blind that I can scarcely see and her I am among the French and Duch and Scoth and Jews and Italions and Sweeds and Chineese and Indians and all manner of tongus and nations but I am treated with due respect by them all.

"I imagine you will say what a long yarn this is from California. if you can read it at all I must close soon for I am so tired and almost sick. Oh my Dear Selden I am so Home sick I will say to you once more to see that Augustus has every thing he kneeds to make him comfortable and by all means have him Dressed warm this cold winter. I worry a great deal about my Dear children. it seems as though my heart would break when I realize how far I am from my Dear Loved ones this from your affectionate mother."

Mary B. Ballou

19

Mother Mary Baptist Russell

Mother Baptiste Russell

She led Sisters of Mercy to California

W hen a priest asked Mother Frances Bridgerman, to select recruits to go to San Francisco in 1854, she hesitated, fearing the women would be scalped.

Despite San Francisco's reputation as a lawless city, twenty-nine Irish Sisters of Mercy volunteered to serve. From that group, Mother Frances chose eight. She selected 26-year-old Sr. Mary Baptist Russell as the group's leader.

Thus, from the Irish seaport town of Kinsale in 1854 came eight young women to a completely different environment, one that was populated with gold prospectors, fortune hunters, and opportunists.

When the Sisters of Mercy arrived in San Francisco December 8, 1854, what they found was jarring. "Gold fever" had hit the men, and many left their wives and children to fend for themselves while they went off to pursue their fortunes.

The exploitation and sale of women were common practices in the roaring city, and the aged and infirm fared little better.

Mother Mary Baptist Russell was determined to help the suffering. One of her first activities was to create a safe haven for women. Under her leadership, the Sisters of Mercy took in abandoned wives and mothers, prostitutes, and naïve young girls. They took in the elderly and began visiting the sick in their homes.

Less than a month after their arrival, the sisters were asked to visit a woman who had just died. While kneeling to pray for the woman, they realized she was not dead. They sent for the priest, revived the woman, and sent her to the county hospital.

Mary Baptist deliberately rented a house near the hospital. Daily the sisters visited the sick, intent on bringing what comfort they could to the patients. At that time, people who went into the hospital rarely left alive.

Patients were left all night in the dark with no water and no one attending them. They had no linen or pillows—they were expected to bring their own if they had any. The nurses in the hospital were people who were not employable anywhere else.

When the 1855 cholera outbreak struck San Francisco, the Sisters of Mercy went to work as nurses in the county hospital. The *San Francisco Daily News* described the sisters' labors during the health crisis:

"A more horrible and ghastly sight we have seldom witnessed. In the midst of this scene of sorrow, pain, anguish, and danger were ministering angels who disregarded everything to aid their distressed fellow creatures. The Sisters of Mercy did not stop to inquire whether the poor sufferers were Protestants or Catholics, Americans or foreigners, but with the noblest devotion applied themselves to their relief."

The cholera disease ultimately killed about five percent of the population.

While Mother Russell's most significant contributions were medical, it was ironic in that she had absolutely no formal medical training. Still, according to the San Francisco Examiner, more than any other single individual, she helped California emerge from the dark ages of hospital care.

Because of their effectiveness during the cholera epidemic, the sisters were asked to take charge of the county hospital. Mother Baptist agreed, but after months of caring for the indigent at the sisters' expense, she told the county it would have to meet its financial obligation to the sisters.

She ended up buying the hospital for $14,000, and when the county built a new hospital, Mother Baptist opened Saint Mary's in 1857, the first Catholic Hospital on the West Coast.

Baptist Russell apparently didn't plan ahead on what she was going to do. She simply experienced reality and then began to build. For instance, she had not planned to build a home for the aged, but when someone came and asked for shelter and there was no place to put her, she began her project for sheltering the infirm aged.

She relied heavily on the providence of God, and often began a project without funding. This prompted one bishop to comment, "Her heart was bigger than her purse."

In 1868, the city was besieged with a different disease outbreak. Smallpox hit the city. The disease was so contagious that even ministers would not visit their dying parishioners.

City officials opened pest houses for those inflicted with the disease. Nurses worked only during the day, leaving victims of smallpox unattended in the darkness from dusk until dawn.

Sr. Mary Baptist asked for and received permission for the sisters to work in the pest houses. For ten months the sisters lived among the smallpox victims.

Mother Baptist worked with atheists, agnostics, bigots, criminals, murderers, as well as those more upstanding. One writer said, "She loved to help people—especially the poor—and in so doing, she became a legend.

She provided wedding dresses for brides too poor to purchase them. She visited men in prisons. She stole from the hospital linen supply to give to the poor. Legend has it that Mother Baptist would pull up her petticoat and wrap the hospital bed linens around her waist and stuff them in her sleeves.

When she reached the home of a needy family, she would pull the linen out and make the beds. She did this so often that the sisters put locks on the linen closets. One time, she pulled her own mattress down the stairs to give it to a poor man.

As good as her works were, she and her Sisters of Mercy had their detractors. An anti-Catholic writer accused the Sisters of mismanaging the hospital and of abusing the patients. In her direct way of getting to the issue, Mother Baptist urged a grand jury investigation into the allegations of the accuser.

The grand jury lauded the hospital as one of three outstanding institutions of San Francisco, along with the schools and the fire department.

Mother Baptist Russell died in August 1898, and thousands came to her funeral. Fr. R.E. Kenna, a Jesuit priest, summed up her life in a letter to the bereaved sisters:

"Gentle as a little child, she was brave and resolute as a crusader. Prudence itself, yet she was fearless in doing good to the needy...all who met her were forced to admire; and those who knew her best loved her most."

School Established in Grass Valley

(Paraphrased from "The Story of Mount Saint Mary's)

In the spring of 1862 Father Thomas J. Dalton, pastor of the thriving community of Grass Valley, applied to the Sisters of Mercy at Saint Mary's Hospital in San Francisco for the founding of a branch house of their order in Grass Valley.

The first request was turned down on the grounds that there were not enough sisters available. Father Dalton was persistent.

In August, he convinced Mother Mary Baptist Russell to make the trip to Grass Valley to judge if it was a place suitable for a house of their order. She did so, accompanied by Sister M. Paul Beechinor and Sister M. Teresa King.

She was immediately surprised by what she saw. A beautiful new brick church had been built and opened on December 5, 1859. It was modeled on the Irish school system.

The Sisters of Mercy Convent in Grass Valley is part of St. Patrick's Church built there in 1858. The Henry Scadden house on the right was first used as an orphanage for small boys and later as a Sisters Chapel.

Mother M. Baptist Russell returned to San Francisco and wrote to Bishop Eugene O'Connell, Vicar Apostolic of Marysville, in whose territory Grass Valley was located.

Several letters were exchanged between the two religious figures, and along with great persuasion from Father Dalton, Mother Baptist Russell agreed to bring a branch of her order to Grass Valley.

The Sisters of Mercy ran the school from 1863 until 1986, when the parish purchased it. It is the oldest Catholic school in continuous operation in California.

(Author's note: Much of this material was first published in the book, "A Call to Care: The Women Who Built Catholic Healthcare in America." The book is now out of print.)

128

20

Donaldina Cameron

She rescued Chinese slave girls

Donaldina Cameron

Donaldina Cameron came to the Presbyterian Mission Home in San Francisco in 1895 to teach sewing to Asian girls and women.

Most of these women were brought to California as slaves. Some were as young as six years of age when the mission rescued them.

They were usually kidnapped, but just as frequently, they were sold by their parents in China, and forced to work as domestics or prostitutes in the United States.

Shortly after Donaldina arrived, her supervisor died. This threw Donaldina, who was twenty-five years old, into the position of director.

She is credited with saving more than three thousand women and children during her forty-seven years at the mission. To those she rescued, she was known as *"White Angel"* and as *"Lo Mo"*, which means Beloved Mother.

Slave dealers and brothel owners did not hold her in such esteem. To them she was *"White Devil"*.

Chinese girls sold by their parents as merchandize to be used in San Francisco brothels.

Often the rescues consisted only of Donaldina and a companion. They would simply walk past the Chinese guards and escort the girls back to the mission. The guards were so confused and surprised at the sight of a white woman in the Chinese ghetto they turned and ran.

Once safely inside the mission, Donaldina and other missionaries helped give the girls a better life. They taught them English and reading and writing—according to their situations. The girls were introduced to Christianity and the Bible, and to cooking, cleaning and sewing.

These women were smuggled into the United States, circumventing immigration laws that excluded them. They were simply commodities that were bought and sold as property. The system was known as the *"yellow slave trade."*

Bogus contracts were created to keep the system working. The contracts were written with insurmountable conditions, making it impossible for the women to purchase their own freedom. Some say the number of Asian women who died in enslaved conditions in San Francisco numbered in the thousands.

Gaining entry into the United States was complicated for the Chinese by the Chinese Exclusion Acts of 1882, 1888, 1892, and 1902 and the Immigration Act of 1924.

These acts increased restrictions on Asian immigrants, especially laborers. Only students, teachers or merchants were admitted to America. The acts were clearly discriminatory, as no other national group was denied entry to the country.

According to Paul Q. Chow, who wrote a thesis on the subject, the fear was that laborers from China would take jobs away from European-American workers. This fear was made worse because of the severe economic depression facing the country at that time.

When Donaldina Cameron, a New Zealand-born Scot, arrived in San Francisco from the San Joaquin Valley, her intention was to devote a "single year" working in the Chinese Presbyterian Mission at 920 Sacramento Street.

When she became aware of the slavery and conditions in Chinatown, she felt repulsed. From a mild-mannered missionary girl, Donaldina was transformed into a zealous social reformer. She became fanatically committed to wiping out the horrors of yellow slavery.

A *San Francisco Examiner* article by Michael Svanevik and Shirley Burgett detailed the lengths to which Cameron would go. "Slavery was a fact of life in China," they wrote. "For centuries, young girls were taught to think of themselves as creatures almost purely for the enjoyment of men and were sold as merchandize to be wives, concubines or prostitutes."

Most of those arriving in California during the gold rush were sold for immoral purposes. State officials were bought off by the Chinese slavers and refused to recognize the existence of the slavery practice.

Most of the girls in San Francisco's Chinatown worked in cribs—narrow cells that accommodated two to six girls. They were required to service all comers, most of whom were white. Patrons paid twenty five to fifty cents for sexual services. Young boys were admitted for fifteen cents.

According to the *San Francisco Examiner*, The Presbyterian Mission spearheaded reform against the yellow slave trade as early as the 1870s. Margaret Culbertson, then the mission's director, instituted raids to liberate captive children.

Donaldina Cameron became Culbertson's assistant in 1895 and assumed the directorship two years later on Culbertson's death.

Cameron became the scourge of the underworld, the *Examiner* wrote. "She came to know every back alley and rooftop in Chinatown. She undertook rescues of young captives who requested assistance or when maltreatment of a child was reported.

When denied access to a crib or parlor, she relied on an unofficial alliance she had developed with San Francisco Police Sergeant Jack Manion, commander of the so-called Chinatown Squad. Manion sympathized with Cameron and ordered his men to "give her whatever she wants."

Police officers in plain clothes gained entry where Cameron could not. They simply pounded down doors with sledgehammers, crowbars and axes.

Plans for such raids were generally kept very secret, but word of them sometimes leaked out and the girls were herded into passageways, tunnels or secret rooms.

The *San Francisco Examiner* noted that Cameron did not limit her activities to San Francisco. She led raids in virtually every city on the Pacific Coast. She admitted that she often found it necessary to "break the letter, though not the spirit, of the law."

Not all girls came to the mission willingly. Many became so frightened at the appearance of Cameron that they jeopardized their own rescues. At least some were forced into the mission against their will.

Police happily assisted Donaldina Cameron in rescuing Chinese slave girls.

"The activities of Cameron and the Presbyterians endangered a very lucrative operation," the *Examiner* reporters explained. "Slave girls represented big money both for the brokers who imported them and for corrupt officials who looked the other way."

During the 1850s, girls sold for between $100 and $500. By the end of World War I, prices had risen to as high as $7,000. Yellow slavery flourished until the 1930s.

The slavery overlords expressed their displeasure with Cameron's crusade. On one occasion, a dynamite bomb was found on the steps of 920

Sacramento Street and disarmed without any damage.

The mission also opened its doors to girls such as Tye Leung, who was born in the United States. Tye lived in a two-room apartment in Chinatown with her mother, father, six brothers and one sister.

Tye's parents arrived before the Chinese Exclusion Acts were enacted. Tye's parents allowed her and her brothers and a sister to adapt American ways. The girls even attended school.

Yet, the father and mother clung to some of their Chinese culture. They selected a bridegroom for their daughter. Tye firmly rejected the idea that she would marry the man her parents had chosen for her.

He was a complete stranger to her and wanted to cart her off to Butte, Montana, a place she knew absolutely nothing about.

Rather than go through with such a marriage, Tye secretly left the home of her mother and father and sought asylum in Donaldina Cameron's mission.

Donaldina Cameron retired in 1938 after forty-seven years with the mission. Four years later, the mission was renamed the Cameron House in her honor. Donaldina Cameron died in 1968 at the age of ninety-eight.

21

The Frightful Journey

While the journey to California's Gold Rush had many scenic splendors, they were greatly outweighed by the hardships.

Lucena Parsons found Chimney Rock in Nebraska a special attraction. Lucy Cooke was struck by the grandeur of the Sweetwater River crashing through Devil's Gate Canyon in Wyoming.

For Mary Medley Ackley, the trip turned especially sour. She saw her mother felled by cholera and buried near the Platte River in Nebraska. "I remember every detail of her death and burial."

Lodisa Frizzell remembered seeing a fresh-made grave, topped by a feather bed. She later learned that a man and his wife had both died a few days earlier and were buried together at that spot. Their two small children were sent back to St. Joseph by an Indian Chief.

Eliza McAuley watched a horrible accident happen. As a wagon came down a steep hill, a woman with a child in her arms tried to jump to safety. Her dress caught in the wheel and she was drawn under and crushed to death.

There was nothing as terrible and grueling as the travel across the great desert. The 40-mile crossing of the blistering sands took its toll on humans, animals and wagons.

The travelers, by the time they reached the desert, had already traveled 1,800 miles. The oxen, mules and horses were worn out and the spirits and bodies of the people were likewise fatigued.

Provisions for most were reduced to starvation levels. There was neither grass nor water available along the road for either humans or livestock.

Luzena Stanley Wilson captured the horror of the desert crossing in her diary in 1849.

"It was a forced march over the alkali plain, lasting three days. We carried with us water that had to last for both men and animals until we reached the other side.

"The hot earth scorched our feet; the grayish dust hung about us like a cloud, making our eyes red, and tongues parched, and our thousand bruises and scratches smarted like burns.

"The road was lined with skeletons of the poor beasts that died in the struggle."

Luzena remembered when two of the wagon train leaders were dying of thirst, not forty yards from her wagon. She took food and water, and "found them bootless, hatless, ragged and tattered, moaning for death to relieve them from their torture. They called me an angel."

Sallie Hester, the daughter of Craven and Martha Hester, recorded the hazardous journey in her diary.

"Had a trying time crossing. Several of our cattle gave out and we left one. Our journey through the desert was from Monday, three o'clock in the afternoon, until Thursday morning at sunrise, September 6.

"The weary journey last night, the mooing of the cattle for water, their exhausted condition, with the cry of 'Another ox down', the stopping of the train to unyoke the poor dying brute, to let him follow at will or stop by the wayside and die, and the weary, weary tramp of men and beasts, worn out with heat and famished for water, will never be erased from my memory."

Margaret and Ledyard Frink endured 37 hours on the frightful desert. Margaret wrote, "For many weeks we had been accustomed to see property abandoned and animals dead or dying.

"But those scenes were doubled and trebled on the desert. Both sides of the road were lined with dead animals and abandoned wagons. Around them were strewed yokes, chains, harness, guns, tools, bedding, clothing and cooking utensils.

"The owners had left everything and hurried on to save themselves. The situation was so desperate that no one could help another. Each had all he could do to save himself and his animals."

22

Packing A Wagon

Nothing was more important to the forty-niners than the choice and kind of supplies they packed in their covered wagons.

They knew it would be a five-month trip. Most wagons carried similar supplies except for the few mementos that children and mothers would sneak into their packing containers.

The wagon was designed more for utility than comfort. The pioneers needed to pack supplies for the entire trip into an area ten feet long by four feet wide.

Most commonly, it was the woman's job to prepare enough food and make enough clothing to supply them for the entire trip.

Weight was a major concern for the travelers. A few extra pounds meant more work for the oxen that pulled the wagons. This was the most common reason that some men and women walked beside the wagon instead of riding inside it.

Each wagon could carry about two-thousand pounds before it became too heavy for the ox team to pull and still traverse the uneven ground across mountains and desert.

The top for most covered wagons was made from linen thread and spun by the woman into a large-enough sheet to cover the wagon. It was common to treat the material with linseed oil or another form of grease to make it waterproof.

A Prairie Schooner

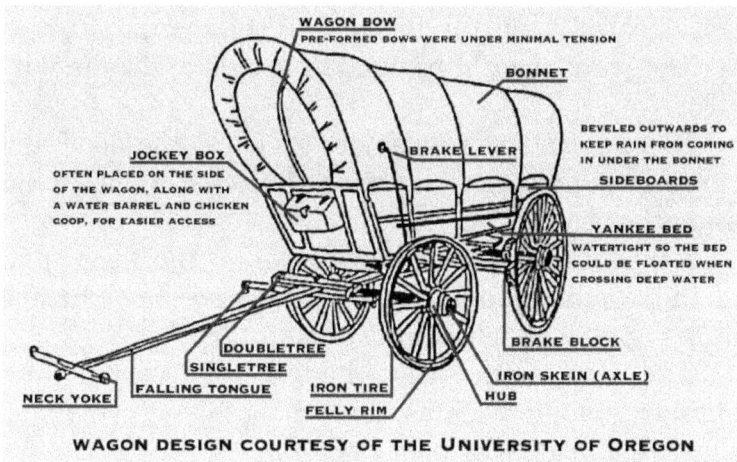

WAGON BOW
PRE-FORMED BOWS WERE UNDER MINIMAL TENSION

BONNET

JOCKEY BOX
OFTEN PLACED ON THE SIDE
OF THE WAGON, ALONG WITH
A WATER BARREL AND CHICKEN
COOP, FOR EASIER ACCESS

BRAKE LEVER

BEVELED OUTWARDS TO
KEEP RAIN FROM COMING
IN UNDER THE BONNET

SIDEBOARDS

YANKEE BED
WATERTIGHT SO THE BED
COULD BE FLOATED WHEN
CROSSING DEEP WATER

DOUBLETREE
SINGLETREE
FALLING TONGUE
NECK YOKE
IRON TIRE
FELLY RIM
BRAKE BLOCK
IRON SKEIN (AXLE)
HUB

WAGON DESIGN COURTESY OF THE UNIVERSITY OF OREGON

The Prairie Schooner was about ten feel long and four feet wide. Provisions for a five month trip were packed into the space.

Overland travelers learned that the large Conestoga wagons were too big for their needs. Even the sturdiest oxen gave out under the weight of the Conestoga.

While many wagons were handmade by the pioneers, Studebaker Brothers and other wainwrights specialized in making a lightweight wagon called the Prairie Schooner. This wagon typically measured four-feet wide and ten to twelve feet in length.

With the "bonnet", or cover, that went over the hoops to form the covered wagon, it could stand close to ten feet tall. Once it was assembled, the empty wagon itself could weigh about thirteen hundred pounds.

The wagon box or "bed" was made of hardwoods to resist shrinking in the dry desert air. The wagon box was about two to three feet deep. The seams were coated with tar to make it watertight. If need be, the wagon could be floated across a slow-moving river.

It was the woman's job to pack the food and clothing supplies, along with the pots, pans, dishes and other things.

Boxes and trunks generally filled the floor space of the wagon, providing a flat surface on which to make up a bed for sleeping at night.

The food items that had to be packed were similar among wagons, but most always included these. Quantities are per person:

200 Pounds of flour
30 pounds of pilot bread (hardtack)
75 pounds bacon
10 pounds rice
5 pounds of coffee
2 pounds of tea
25 pounds of sugar
1/2 bushel dried beans

1 bushel of dried fruit

2 pounds of saleratus (baking soda)

10 pounds of salt

1/2 bushel of corn meal

1/2 bushel of corn, parched and ground

1 small keg of vinegar

One other important item mentioned in most dairies was the inclusion of the "India rubber water bottle". Some wagons even carried India rubber water mattresses which could be used to store drinking water as well as provide a mattress to sleep on.

Besides the food supplies, room had to be made to carry tools that would be needed on the trip. Included were an axe (15 pounds); shovel (12 pounds); hatchet (nine pounds); hammer (7 pounds); hoe (3 pounds); anvil (150 pounds) grinding stone (75 pounds); and an animal trap, (15 pounds) and rope (4 pounds).

There were a number of personal items that needed to be packed and estimated as far as weight.

For instance, this list might include: a doll, a jump rope, marbles, family Bible, books, hunting knife, a bag of cloths, a fiddle, snowshoes, rifle, pistol, and a first aid kit.

There was considerable furniture to pack, sometimes including a piano or organ that someone in the family cherished. Miscellaneous goods might include a coffee grinder, a rug, a mirror, a Dutch oven, a butter churn, table and chairs, baby cradle, a bed pan and a butter mold.

If there was room, a rocking chair might be packed, a pitcher and a bowl, cooking utensils, a spinning wheel, a lantern, 10 candles, a clock and a set of dishes.

Oxen were generally used to pull the covered wagons as they could survive longer without water than could horses.

The only set of springs on a Prairie Schooner was underneath the seldom-used driver's seat.

Some stretches of the trail were so rough that a churn could be filled with fresh cream in the morning and it would bounce around enough to churn a lump of butter.

Not all emigrants had the luxury of the "factory-made" Prairie Schooners. Some pioneers simply used farm wagons, which were smaller and not as well sheltered, as the Prairie Schooner.

23

Curse of the Gold Mines

The gold mines have ever been a curse and a drawback in this country. Prices of labor do not correspond with the prices of our produce…How can farmers afford to pay $40 per month for second rate hands, fifty dollars for common two horse harness, twenty-five dollars for a two-horse plow, twelve cents a bushel for threshing grain—and sell their wheat at 75 cents, oats 40 cents, potatoes 25 cents, pork 5 to 6 cents, onions $1, peas 75 cents, etc. etc.

I pay sawyers on my mill $60 per month, log choppers $40 to $50 and yet I sell weatherboards at $12 per thousand feet! Hence, many, very many, will vote for slavery in order to cheapen labor!

(David Newsom 1857)

24

Property Rights

In the 1849 Constitutional Convention, delegates took up the issue of women's property rights.

One question discussed at length and with enthusiasm was whether the property held by a woman at the time of her marriage should be reserved for her and protected from her husband by a specific code in the Constitution.

Delegates, speaking to the issue, advanced two cogent arguments on behalf of the provision. The delegate from San Luis Obispo, Henry Tefft, cited existing laws, in which Mexican civil law guaranteed native California women separate property rights.

James M. Jones, the Stockton delegate, argued that marriage constituted a civil contract, a partnership in which both parties shared equally.

Henry Hallack, a Monterey delegate was rebuked for his argument, best judged as enlightened self-interest. This is the argument Hallack put forth:

> *"Having some hopes that sometime or other I may be wedded...I shall advocate this section in the Constitution, and I would call upon all the bachelors in this Convention to vote for it. I do not think we can offer a greater inducement for women of fortune to come to California. It is the very best provision to get us wives."*

Charles Botts vigorously opposed the provision before the convention. His argument was:

> *"There must be a master in every household. A woman takes her husband for better, for worse; that is the position in which she voluntarily places herself, and it is not for you to withdraw her from it. I beg you, I entreat you, not to lay the rude hand of legislation upon this beautiful, and poetical position."*

Delegate Jones of Stockton effectively countered Botts' argument.

> *"What is the principal so much glorified, but that the husband shall be a despot, and the wife shall have no right but such as he chooses to award her. It had its origin in a barbarous age, when the wife was considered in the light of a menial, and had no rights. In this age of civilization, it has been found that the wife has certain rights."*

Pioneer woman Eliza Farnham married such a despot. Fortunately, her mistake was easily rectified. Santa Cruz County granted her one of its first divorces and she prepared to return East with Charles, he only surviving son.

25

Disputes Along the Way

As might be expected, with so many people involved, all was not peace and tranquility among wagon train travelers.

Rachel Taylor heard: "…another quarrel among our neighbors and one which will not be so easily settled. It seems that Will sold his Uncle a yoke of cattle and now refused to give them up." Rachel said he used abusive language to his uncle and aunt.

More serious was the event reported by Celinda Hine three weeks later. "Several trains traveled near us," she wrote. "In one was a lady who was recently married. Her husband set her out of the [unreadable] wagon giving her [unreadable]."

Another company took her in and liked her very much. The husband in the dispute said his wife was ugly to his children, she being his second wife.

Sarah Davis described another incident that happened in July 1850 that was even more serious. It was a Sunday.

"A large train come in one mile of us and camped. There arose a quarrel with them and what quarreling I never heard the like of. The men were whipping a man for whipping his wife. He had whipped her every day since he joined the company. Now they thought it was time for them to whip him. They stripped him and took the ox goad to him and whipped him tremendous."

Three years earlier, Elizabeth Dixon Smith observed an even more unusual incident.

"One Mrs. Markham became angry and refused to budge one morning when it was time for the company to begin its day's travel. Three hours of coaxing from her husband had no apparent effect, so 'neighbors' took the couples' children into their wagons.

"The wife then got up and backtracked and took a short cut, overtaking her husband's wagon.

"In the meantime he had sent their son back for a horse which had been left. When the wife rejoined him, he asked her if she had met John. She said yes, and 'I picked up a stone and nocked out his brains'

"The concerned husband went back to ascertain the truth. His wife had set one of his wagons on fire which was loaded with store

153

goods. The wagon cover was burned off as well as some articles.

"When the husband saw the flame he was able to run and put it out and then gave his wife a good flogging."

Whatever truly happened, the boy did not get his brains 'nocked' out.

Lucretia Lawson Epperson cites another disagreeable incident between wagon train members.

She said her company met a man looking for his wife. While he went to Virginia City for supplies, his wife sold the ranch, purchased two horses and a wagon and started for Illinois. He wanted to know if the Epperson's had seen her.

We told him we had met her over fifty miles back. The deserted husband sighed and said, "Well, I will let her go, as I could not overtake her before reaching Salt Lake." He turned about and started westward.

E.W. Conyers tells about his party meeting up with a widow who had just buried her husband. She had four or five children to care for. Her company had gone on, leaving her alone with her team and little ones.

She had three yoke of cattle and her wagon. "When we overtook her, she was driving wooden wedges between the tires of the six wagon wheels. After we repaired her wagon wheels, the widow declined an offer of further assistance.

"She picked up her whip, gave it a whirl and a crack and started down the mountain."

Conyers said, "We did not see her or hear anything more about her after leaving the summit."

26

Wagon Train Medicine

In 1826, in the northeast Indian province of Bengal, a microscopic curved rod, the bacillus Vibrio cholera, began eating human intestines. The disease worked quickly, killing fifty percent of its hosts.

The disease was diagnosed as cholera. Cholera was spread primarily by contaminated water and by flies that carry contamination from fecal matter to food.

Unwittingly, immigrants and traders carried the bacillus from India. In time it found its way to the port of New York, spread north and south on the east coast of the United States and then moved westward.

It was carried by trappers and soldiers and the wagon trains of early pioneers, contaminating streams and water holes along the way. By 1834, it reached the Pacific Coast.

When Utah's pioneer set off on their westward trek, Vibrio cholera went with them. So did the bacteria of typhoid, diphtheria, tuberculosis, scarlet fever, and whooping cough.

The diary and journal entries recording death and sickness along the pioneer trails, such as in the California Gold Rush, are wrenching to read.

Writer Joan Shaw issued a report detailing some of the wretched results of these contagious diseases.

"I helped lay out six children, dead of diphtheria," said Margaret Elzirah Rawlins, Relief Society President in Lewiston, Utah.

Pioneer medicines had to travel well and not take up too much room in a covered wagon.

The pioneers concocted their own nostrums in an attempt to stem the tide of the diseases. Among the home remedies mentioned by medical historians were mixtures of pungent herbs or turpentine mixed with lard—and in one case—a split chicken—applied to the chest for respiratory distress.

Often new cures had to be found for ailments the pioneers had not encountered before leaving their homes and hitting the trail. At times, the plants, herbs and other ingredients comprising the supposed cure seemed more harmful that the ailment.

Honey, red pepper and butter were used for sore throat. Assorted syrups containing vinegar, molasses and whiskey were used for coughs.

In 1868, Nancy Kerr administered dried chicken gizzards as a deterrent to vomiting to seven-year-old Mary Eveline Rawlins, who suffered from cholera. Authorities say the fact the child lived could be a testimonial for dried chicken gizzards to settle the stomach, though the dose might seem to modern minds to have the opposite effect.

Pioneers dealt with medicine the best way a migratory group could. They packed only the herbs and solutions that would travel well without taking up too much room. They relied on the land to supply the rest.

Patent medicines were often relied upon in the scarce world of medical treatment. These panaceas in a bottle most often contained alcohol, cocaine, opium, or morphine that would temporarily deaden pain and give the illusion of health.

One of the biggest and most mysterious diseases for emigrants was cholera. A person with cholera could go from healthy to dead in just a few hours.

Sometimes the patients were given a proper burial, but often, the sick would be abandoned, in their beds, on the side of the trail. They would die alone.

Making matters worse, were the animals that dug up the dead and scattered the trail with human bones and body parts.

The perils of an accident while emigrating west could be devastating with no doctors around.

Cholera killed more emigrants than any other disease. In some years, wagon trains lost two-thirds of their people.

One pioneer woman said, "No one should travel this road without medicine, for they are sure to have the summer complaint. Each family should have "physicking" pills, a quart of castor oil, a quart of the best rum, and a large vial of peppermint essence.

One of the realities of the 1800s was that one in six children did not live to adulthood. People hurt in wagon accidents ran a high risk of tetanus or complications. Appendicitis was often fatal.

People born with birth defects such as harelip, cleft palate, club foot, bone malformations and eye problems learned to live with their conditions.

For people with rotting teeth, pulling was the only remedy. Tooth brushes were not available in stores until the 1830s, but were not widely used until dental hygiene was taught in schools.

One example of misguided thinking, hydrocephalus involved an abnormal accumulation of fluid on the brain in children. The problem was then called "dropsy of the brain". It was thought the disease was caused by trying to excessively stimulate a child's intellect.

One of the cures was to shave the child's head, and cover it with a poultice of onions stewed in vinegar.

27

Women First to Find Gold

'Flakes of gold clung to their laundry'

It may have been three women who first discovered gold in California. Their discovery is dated a full year before James Marshall discovered gold at Sutter's Mill in Coloma, a discovery that attracted hordes of gold seekers to California.

The women were Mrs. Adna Hecox, Mrs. Joseph Aram, and Mrs. Isaac Isbell. They were part of a wagon train coming to California from the mid-west. It was while doing laundry in a tributary stream of the Yuba River that the ladies noticed the glittering flakes clinging to their towels and sheets.

Mrs. Hecox, who tells of the experience in her book, *"California Caravan"*, said she gathered several of the shiny specks of glitter into her apron. When she showed them to her minister husband, he guffawed, telling her she was foolhardy. In a fit of woman's temper, Mrs. Hecox tossed her flakes to the wind.

Mrs. Aram, doing her laundry further downstream shouted to the other women to hurry over. "I do believe I have found gold," she declared. She held up a nugget the size of a dime. She tucked the nugget away until the wagon train arrived at Sutter's Fort in Sacramento.

There, the nugget was assayed, and was indeed pure gold.

While the men in the wagon train marked the site of Mrs. Aram's find, hoping to one day return and search for more gold, none ever came back.

"This country was in such a tumult at the time," wrote Mrs. Hecox, "that people had little opportunity to search for gold until affairs were in a more settled condition and the people were out of danger."

Had the women's discovery of gold in the Yuba River tributary in 1846 been heralded as loudly as that of James Marshall a year later at Coloma, history might indeed have been written differently.

28

Gold Rush Dresses

A truly Victorian Dress

From the Gold Museum Collection

1871 Women's Fashions

The Curtain Lady

A Wedding Dress

29

She Sold Dogs to Miners

Among the first settlers in what is now called Magalia, formerly "Dogtown" was the Bassett family. The story of how Dogtown got its name dates back to the early Gold Rush days.

Located in northern California, Dogtown was established as a gold mining camp shortly after the 1849 California Gold Rush. It sat on a ridge overlooking the West Branch of the Feather River Canyon.

According to the Territorial Quarterly, Robert Stuart and his two sons, Granville and James, came to California from Iowa in 1852 to prospect for gold. On arriving in California, they traveled up through Bidwell's Bar in Butte County.

They continued through Morris Ravine, finally arriving at Sam Neal's Rancho. Granville Stuart recorded his account of Neal's Rancho and Dogtown.

"We spent a week at Sam Neal's ranch in the Sacramento Valley, but as every meal we ate cost each of us a dollar, James and I determined to leave and go up into the mountains to the gold mines.

"We went 16 miles up in the foothills to a little village on the ridge between the West Branch of the Feather River and Little Butte Creek.

"This little village was known as Butte Mills because of a saw mill nearby run by water power from Little Butte Creek.

"The village soon got its proper and well-deserved name of Dogtown, for although there were only ten houses, there were sixteen fully developed dogs."

According to various historic accounts, Mrs. Bassett had neither horse nor wagon among her possessions when she arrived at the tiny camp overlooking the West Branch of the Feather River Canyon.

Mrs. Bassett did have with her three undistinguished dogs, one male and two females.

She decided to pitch a tent overlooking the Feather River and try her luck at gold panning. "She was a tough old gal, but no miner," Stuart said. She had to find other ways to get by.

Her good fortune came soon after she arrived. Her pups multiplied and saved her day.

Many of the gold miners left their families at home and grew very lonely, wanting some kind of companionship. Mrs. Bassett recognized their need.

She sold her puppies to the gold miners for a large pinch of gold dust each. Soon every cabin along the ridge had a canine companion.

Stuart said, "There were dogs in the stores, dogs in the saloons, dogs everywhere. It's no wonder that strangers to the area remarked, 'This must be Dogtown'!"

Until 1859, Dogtown remained known only to the locals and most probably they preferred it that way. But in April 1859, a gigantic 54 pound gold nugget was discovered on the slopes of Sawmill Peak, just across the canyon of the West Branch of the Feather River from Dogtown.

It was dubbed the "Dogtown Nugget". It started a new gold rush to the area.

A.K. Stearns, a workman, found the gold nugget in the Willard Claim, a hydraulic mine owned by three miners, Willard, Wetherbee, and Smith. The nugget was later valued at $10,690.

At today's prices, estimates put the value of the nugget at more than $350,000. Reports claim a 96-ounce nugget was found on the same site in 1854.

This rich piece of ore was dubbed the "Dogtown Nugget" and made the headlines of newspapers across the United States. The news started a small gold rush of its own to the Dogtown area.

The women in Dogtown didn't appreciate their town's name. They resented having to write "Dogtown" on their letters to family and friends back home.

It cost two dollars for postage to send a letter from Marysville to Dogtown and took up to three weeks for delivery.

On August 16, 1860, The *Marysville Appeal* ran a letter from one of the discontented wives living in Dogtown.

"We should hate to live in a place called 'Dogtown', particularly if we had a large

correspondence and had to write the name frequently."

The women of Dogtown waged a strong campaign to change the name. After much discussion, Dogtown was renamed "Magalia", the Latin word for "cottages". The Magalia name was apparently adopted for the Magalia mine that was discovered in the area in 1855.

Large-scale mining continued in Dogtown, or Magalia, until the 1890s.

30

Olive Mann Isbell

T here were 23 covered wagons at Fort Hall in eastern Idaho, when an ominous message arrived. President Polk had just declared war on Mexico.

The question for the pioneers going to California was, "Should we go ahead, or should we turn back?"

Among the covered wagon pioneers were Olive Mann Isbell and her husband, Dr. Isaac Chauncey Isbell. They were from Greenbush, Illinois and headed to California.

"What shall we do Olive?" asked her husband.

"I started for California and I want to go on," she said, not hesitating. Her words strengthened the resolve of some of the others in the pioneering group. While some did turn back, others decided to forge ahead.

The company of pioneers spent two weeks making roads and devising ways to get their wagons across the brutal Sierra Nevada Mountains. They wanted to get the wagons across without taking them apart.

When the party descended at the head of the Bear River, both people and animals were exhausted. On October 1, 1846, they arrived at Johnson's Ranch.

"Can you tell us," they asked, "how much farther we shall have to travel to reach California?"

"You are in California now," a smiling Johnson informed them.

An officer of Colonel John C. Fremont escorted the party to Sutter's Fort, and a week later, to Santa Clara Mission for the winter.

The future wasn't bright for the settlers. The soldiers of Don Francisco Sanchez appeared ready to attack the mission at any moment.

Only a few of the American settlers remained at the mission. All of the men were drafted to fight with Colonel Fremont's army.

Mrs. Isbell recognized that the 20 children at the mission needed attention. She was a former school teacher herself and her first thought for children was a school.

With help from the children and other volunteers, a 15-foot square adobe stable was cleared and cleaned. A rickety table and a few benches were made from scraps of wood found in the compound.

The roof leaked and the earthen floor was damp and wet. When heat was needed, a fire was built on a stone platform in the center of the room.

Textbooks were few, and there were no pencils or slates. Lacking a blackboard, Mrs. Isbell scratched lessons on the dirt floor with a long pointed stick.

She wrote the youngster's A-B-Cs on the palms of the pupil's hands with a piece of charcoal. The children called her Aunt Olive.

This was the first school in California taught by an American.

Marines from Yerba Buena (now San Francisco) arrived with some supplies. Thirty-two armed troops ventured out into an adjacent field to wait for Don Francisco's horsemen. He was seeking revenge for the pillage of his rancho by Americanos.

A formal treaty signed on January 7 ended the campaign in Northern California during the Mexican War.

Dr. Isbell, who was with Fremont's army, contracted what was called "typhoid pneumonia". He returned to the Santa Clara Mission. His wife nursed him along with others who had the fever.

The doctor's well-filled medicine chest and Olive's nursing skills kept the death rate low. She gave out more than 100 doses of medicine a day.

It was learned that the Mexicans had concealed kegs of gunpowder in the mission, planning to blow it up. A messenger was sent to the American troops in San Jose.

Twenty-five marines were dispatched from Yerba Buena. As they approached the mission, their cannon bogged down in the mud. Mrs. Isbell loaned the marines her handkerchief to use as a flag of truce while they pulled their cannon from the mud.

The Isbells moved to Monterey where the doctor set up a medical practice. Word of Mrs. Isbell's success as a schoolteacher preceded their arrival. She was called upon to open a school in Monterey.

Her classroom was located in a large room above the jail. The initial enrollment was 25 students, but quickly jumped to 56. Tuition was $6 each for six months.

The Isbells ended up settling in Santa Paula, California. In 1926, a school in Santa Paula was named for Olive Isbell.

Index

178

179

180

Meet the Author

Alton Pryor

Alton Pryor has published fifty-plus books since turning 70 in 1997—many of them about California's past and the colorful characters who rode our trails to fame or infamy.

To date he has sold more than 300,000 copies of his first book, "Little Known Tales in California History", and has done respectably well with most of his other titles.

But until fate derailed his 33-year journalism career, he never aspired to write a book, and certainly never anticipated he would come to be regarded as "Mr. Self-Publishing" by his peers in the Sacramento area. "I would have liked living in the Old West," he says. "I wanted, at one time, to be a really good cowboy. I had horses as a young man and even took a raw colt and trained it to work cattle."

But, by the time Pryor was born on March 19, 1927, the era of gunslingers and gold miners was over, and he started life, instead, on his family's farm outside of King City in the Salinas Valley.

He actually hated farm work. And yet, after 4-years in the Navy, he enrolled at Cal Poly, San Luis Obispo. His major: Agricultural Writing.

"I liked meeting and talking with farmers. I just didn't want to do their dirty work."

He was terminated after writing for 27 years for California Farmer magazine. The magazine was sold to a Midwest firm.

Pryor turned to writing books and says now, "I wish I had been fired 20 years earlier."

www.ingramcontent.com/pod-product-compliance
Lightning Source LLC
LaVergne TN
LVHW021447080426
835509LV00018B/2187